The Luxury of Daydreams

The Luxury of Daydreams

Amy McVay Abbott

*To Jerry and Penny —
Follow your joy
Amy McVay Abbott*

Copyright © 2011 Amy McVay Abbott.

All rights reserved. No part of this book may be used or reproduced by any means, graphic, electronic, or mechanical, including photocopying, recording, taping or by any information storage retrieval system without the written permission of the publisher except in the case of brief quotations embodied in critical articles and reviews.

The cover is an original work in oil by artist Barbara Fox Borries, Evansville, IN March 2011

Scripture taken from the HOLY BIBLE, NEW INTERNATIONAL VERSION®. Copyright © 1973, 1978, 1984 Biblica. Used by permission of Zondervan. All rights reserved.

WestBow Press books may be ordered through booksellers or by contacting:

WestBow Press
A Division of Thomas Nelson
1663 Liberty Drive
Bloomington, IN 47403
www.westbowpress.com
1-(866) 928-1240

Because of the dynamic nature of the Internet, any web addresses or links contained in this book may have changed since publication and may no longer be valid. The views expressed in this work are solely those of the author and do not necessarily reflect the views of the publisher, and the publisher hereby disclaims any responsibility for them.

Any people depicted in stock imagery provided by Thinkstock are models, and such images are being used for illustrative purposes only.

Certain stock imagery © Thinkstock.

ISBN: 978-1-4497-1948-7 (sc)
ISBN: 978-1-4497-1949-4 (e)

Library of Congress Control Number: 2011931841

Printed in the United States of America

WestBow Press rev. date: 6/30/2011

For Randy

May the God of Hope

fill you with all joy and peace

as you trust in Him.

Romans 15:13

Table of Contents

	Acknowledgements	xi
	Introduction	xiii
Chapter 1	Quiet. Be Still!	1
Chapter 2	The Blue Bowl	5
Chapter 3	What I Did For Love	9
Chapter 4	A Single Mother in Hard Times	13
Chapter 5	Requiem and Release	19
Chapter 6	Sweatshirt Weather	23
Chapter 7	Goodbye, Gum Street	27
Chapter 8	The Rhythm of Saturday	31
Chapter 9	Field of Dreams	33
Chapter 10	The Pizza Boy	37
Chapter 11	Lessons from My Son's First Job	41
Chapter 12	Mug Shots	43
Chapter 13	The Sounds of Mothering	47
Chapter 14	I'm Deaf and Dying	51
Chapter 15	Cleaning Her House	55
Chapter 16	B – I – N – G – Zero !!!	59
Chapter 17	The Third Piano	65
Chapter 18	The Bloody Fourth of July	69
Chapter 19	Through a Glass, Darkly	73
Chapter 20	The Trip to Rowena	77
Chapter 21	Built on the Rock	83
Chapter 22	Working on Christmas Eve	87
Chapter 23	Remembering 9/11	91
Chapter 24	Letter to my Seventeen-Year-Old Self	95
Chapter 25	Pet Sounds	99

Chapter 26	Like Birds in Flight	103
Chapter 27	Hester Little Adams	105
Chapter 28	What Matters Most	111
Chapter 29	Guernsey Field Day and Other Humiliations	115
Chapter 30	A 1967 Christmas Story	119
Afterword	On Our Way Rejoicing	125
About the Author	Amy McVay Abbott	127

Acknowledgements

Every creative person needs a healthy ego. A voice deep inside makes us eager to share our muse, and believe others will find meaning in our words, art, or music.

This journey of daydreams has been a joy for me. Without the love and grace of many individuals, this book could not be a reality.

Much gratitude and love to my dear husband, Randy Abbott, who has put up with me for more than a quarter of a century. He is the best man I know and provides love and encouragement that buoys me in the waters of life. He is also a fine writer and editor, and I am grateful to him for his coaching.

To my father and mother, William and Marilyn McVay, thank you for teaching me to appreciate true beauty. From my father I learned to see the spectrum of blue in a summer sky; from my mother I learned to see the grace and beauty in all people. I recognize and bless the legacy of all four of my grandparents, Carl and LeNore Enz, and William and Myrtle McVay. I also honor the memory of my dear mother-in-law Wilma Abbott.

To our son, Alex Abbott, thank you for the joy and laughter you have brought into our lives.

To my editor, Ruth Stanley, thank you for giving me a chance to write after a thirty-year hiatus. Your encouragement and professional guidance means more to me than you could possibly know.

To my prayer partner, Donna Whitenack, thank you for your special support of this book.

To all of my friends, thank you for your encouragement, especially: Therese Asher, Barbara Borries, Rita Bourland, Ann Colbert, Bill and

Darlene Conklin, Cathie Dunigan, Lynda Heines, Julia Jacobs, Cheryl Edwards Martin, Charlene Mires, Carla Sheeler Mitchell, Anne Shrock Ott, Maureen O'Connor Shepherd, MD Walters, and Jean Wilfong Howell.

To my online writing group—The Rules Committee—thank you for teaching me, encouraging me, challenging me, and making me laugh.

Finally, I offer my gratitude and this book to God, who makes all things possible.

Amy McVay Abbott
April 2011
Newburgh, Indiana

Introduction

Losing my job six months after my only child left home for college gave me an unexpected gift, the return of a voice long silenced.

As a child, I was a daydreamer. Adults pegged me as someone with a wild imagination, someone who constantly exaggerated.

Flying off on fanciful trips like Peter Pan across the London night sky, I lived inside my head. To encourage my imagination, my mother shared poems and great children's literature. She also gave me her college typewriter, a portable Royal, when I was six years old. I pounded out stories and poems.

In high school and college, I anticipated a career as a storyteller and mistress of words. I worked on my high school newspaper, college yearbook, and interned at a daily newspaper. Life moved me in another career direction. Writing in the business world tapped out my creative well. Managing a full-time job and raising a child with Asperger's Syndrome overrode daydreaming and wild imagination. I could not dance in my head when I had to stand in reality.

In January 2009, I lost my job six months after my son left home for a university a thousand miles away.

My husband and I were alone in a quiet house.

To my surprise, a voice exploded in my head. One minute I was filing expense reports and helping with Boy Scouts, and the next minute I was time traveling in my head, seeing the world anew through my lifetime of experiences.

Now, I have crested the apex of life's bell curve. My welcome daydreams shepherd me through my own life and the lives of loved ones who came before me.

These essays reflect my thoughts on faith and family, love and laughter, and speak to the issues women of a certain age encounter. These stories depict a light-hearted and sometimes candid view of reality. At certain points in the book, I have changed names, places, and dates to protect privacy.

When I am time traveling, I sometimes rediscover a familiar scene that is lost in my own imagination, like the child me wandering on a playground.

I stop and jot my impressions into an ever-present notebook, confident the words will be there.

The French call this state of being *reverie*.

Whatever it is, my daydreaming is a luxury, a way to bridge memories of a lifetime with hope and faith in the future.

It is indeed a lovely gift.

Quiet. Be Still!

Chapter 1

That day when evening came, he said to his disciples, "Let us go over to the other side." Leaving the crowd behind, they took him along, just as he was, in the boat. There were also other boats with him. A furious squall came up, and the waves broke over the boat, so that it was nearly swamped. Jesus was in the stern, sleeping on a cushion. The disciples woke him and said to him, "Teacher, don't you care if we drown?" He got up, rebuked the wind and said to the waves, "Quiet! Be still!" Then the wind died down and it was completely calm. He said to his disciples, "Why are you so afraid? Do you still have no faith?"

They were terrified and asked each other, "Who is this? Even the wind and the waves obey him!"

Mark 4:35-41

Our family periodically visits Seagrove Beach on the Panhandle of Florida. The sun, sea, and sand rejuvenate my soul, and renew all that is within me. I enjoy walking on the Gulf's edge, standing in the water and moving against the incoming waves, or lazing in an Adirondack chair while scanning the horizon for nothing in particular.

During a 2006 visit to Seagrove, I stood at the water's edge, squished my toes into the white, sugary sands, and watched sand and water rush around my feet. To avoid the relentless waves knocking me down, I dug my feet into the sand. With my feet buried, I was lodged against the unceasing water.

How firm my foundation!

A Gulf of Mexico beach is the perfect place for reflection. Like some eccentric character from literature in my purple madras shorts, pink beach hat, and holey T-shirt, I stood at the water's edge and had an epiphany.

Life is just like this beach.

As I stood on that beach, I pondered my upcoming fiftieth birthday. I know there will be many waves crashing upon me in the coming years. Dig in as I might, the waves will be relentless. The sand around my feet may dissolve. My firm stance may disappear without something larger or greater on which to hold.

I recently reread the story about Jesus' disciples in a boat on the Sea of Galilee. I thought about my moment on the beach. I thought about Jesus sleeping calmly in a wooden boat with wicked, ten-foot swells beating all around.

His disciples were distracted with fear while Jesus slept. They awakened their Teacher and asked wryly if he happened to notice they were "perishing."

Jesus stood up in the boat and "rebuked the wind, and said to the sea, 'Quiet. Be still'!"

The churning sea immediately stilled.

Let us review. Disciples who gave up hearth and home to follow their new leader had little faith in Him. Even in the physical presence of Christ, they lacked faith to trust Him for personal safety.

This is a great object lesson for a post-menopausal beachcomber wearing a quirky, hot pink hat.

Storms rage over us every day. Sometimes I can see the showers coming at me full force, and I dig my heels in deep. Sometimes the rains sneak up on me. Like the waves, storms are unending, part of the rhythms and tides of our lives.

Often the crushing waves coming toward us—on beach or boat—are terrifying and overwhelming. The loss of a spouse or other loved one, divorce, financial upheaval, loneliness, and illness are larger versions of the disciples' fears.

We need to trust that Jesus is beside us among the squalls and thunder boomers. We need to listen with open hearts to hear Him say, "Quiet. Be still!"

The Blue Bowl

Chapter 2

*P*ictures often do not tell the full story of a life. In my living room, I have framed wedding pictures of both sets of my mother's grandparents. Like many turn-of-the-last-century nuptial photographs, the couples stand stiff and solemn, no nuptial joy visible on their faces.

My mother as a 1955 bride closely resembled her grandmother, Anna Long Hoard, as Anna looked in her 1898 bridal portrait. The pictures reveal petite, dark-haired beauties. Is this resemblance between grandmother and granddaughter any clue to who my great-grandmother was?

Who was this young woman—Anna—who lived and died on the same farm that her grandfather settled in 1830? What did she see in my great-grandfather Henry Kellis Hoard? How did she meet the man who was called Kellis? What traits did she pass on to her three daughters? How did Anna cope when her oldest daughter Sara May died tragically in an accident, thrown from her fiancé's yellow coupe?

I recently received a package from my aunt that answered questions and hinted at others. At eighty-plus, my aunt is cataloging and sharing a lifetime of family treasures.

The package contained a beautiful quilt, described by my aunt as "grandmother's flower garden." She said it is a traditional quilt pattern.

Great-grandmother Anna pieced the top squares together in the 1930s. Anna died in 1936, when my mother was four and my aunt was eight.

The "quilting bee" was a favorite social activity for women of Tunker, a farm village in northeast Indiana. After the quilt blocks were joined and sandwiched with batting and backing, friends and neighbors secured the quilt to a frame.

After the quilt was completed, Anna tucked it in a cedar chest for her granddaughter, my aunt. Eighty years after creation, this lovely treasure came to me, via my aunt in Massachusetts, back home again in Indiana.

I knew the quilt was coming, but another object in the package took me completely by surprise. My aunt included a simple blue pottery bowl. The bowl is like many I have owned and has no significant value as a piece of art or as an antique.

Nevertheless, as the commercial says, the value to me is priceless.

My aunt's memories of my great-grandmother making noodles in this bowl is the real gift.

From my aunt's letter: *"Grandma was a good cook. Her 'cuisine' was simple, homegrown, but tasty and healthy. I have her blue pottery mixing bowl, which I will also send to you. It is part of a dear memory for me. I remember Grandma taking the yolks from the chicken eggs she had gathered and cleaned and mixing them with water, salt, and flour to make yellow noodle dough. She rolled the dough out very thin, let it dry a little and then rolled it and sliced off noodles, which were then spread out to dry and later cooked. I thought Grandma was just a wonder."*

My aunt's letter offered me a vivid picture of my great-grandmother making noodles for her daughter, son-in-law, and two granddaughters.

Great-grandmother's hands sewed the quilt, which has had only light use during the past eighty years. The blue bowl was something Anna used every day. It represents an intimate connection to a woman who died twenty-three years before I was born. Holding this bowl, most likely purchased for a few dollars at a dry goods store, connects me to this woman I never knew.

What I Did For Love

Chapter 3

Parenting is not for sissies. We do things for our children that we will do for no one else. I rise up on the proverbial high horse, kvetching over the torment I experienced in the name of my only child.

Childbirth itself is a gruesome affair where the guest of honor is woefully indifferent to the hostess. Like Queen Victoria, I was not amused with the act of delivering an eight-pound baby with a melon-sized head. Every vein in my face bulged; each photograph showed a red-faced mother and a sleeping, perfect baby, who is oblivious to the love showered upon him.

The hospital served the proud mama and papa a filet mignon dinner. I could not sit still from the pain. The proud father of my child pointed at my filet with his fork and said, "Mind if I eat that?" as I grimaced in pain and squirmed in the plastic hospital chair at St. Marquis de Sade Memorial Hospital and Torture Chamber.

Parenting involved sleepless nights, teething, his first day of school anxiety, my anxiety when he went to church camp, his learning to parallel park, and my anxiety and tears over his first days at college.

We, as his parents, made sacrifices. My lifelong dream is to visit

Italy. We sent <u>him</u> when he was seventeen. While our desire for him to have these experiences is genuine, I ask. "What is wrong with this picture?"

All parents give up things, large and small. We gave up our view from the St. Louis Gateway Arch when Mother Nature left her calling card in our son's diaper. In retrospect, it was poor judgment to schlep an eighteen-month-old baby to the top of the Gateway Arch.

"We don't need to take the diaper bag with us. We will not be gone that long," I said to my dear husband, shortly before we bought our tickets. I spoke these words just as we approached the line to board the little cars to the top.

Gentility prevents me from further describing exactly what the child did right before the trip to the top of the Arch. However, I will report that US Steel, engineers of the arch, would have been impressed over the scope and dimensions of his project. We had already bought our too-expensive tickets, and waited in a long line for the tiny five-person elevator. Let your imagination run wild, with all your senses.

Do you remember Chevy Chase as Clark Griswold at the Grand Canyon in *National Lampoon's Vacation*? Now, picture him hoisting a thirty-pound baby with a fifteen-pound diaper.

We rode to the top, raced to one side, raced to the other side, and immediately jumped back in line for the smelly trip down. Our son, Old Poopinguts, smiled and laughed a goofy, gap-toothed grin at his appalled parents and the other hostages in the elevator.

After the slow descent, our elevator mates climbed quickly over us for a clean getaway.

Diaper days eventually ended, especially when the child was finally potty trained. I lacked the necessary knowledge; so, my husband provided on-the-job training for our son.

The child grew. So grew the need for cold, hard cash—money for college, teeth, speech therapy, a baritone horn, Scout trips to Space

Camp and whitewater rafting, money for this, money for that. Nothing I have described seems over the top for parents. We do the best we can for our children with what we have. We accept it as the nature of the beast—beast being a relative term.

Nothing about my role as a mother seemed unreasonable until I heard a recent news item. Numerous media outlets reported that research has determined moderate amounts of caffeine during pregnancy will not harm a fetus.

Are you kidding me? More than two decades ago, popular wisdom within the medical community was that caffeine was poison to a fetus. Let me tell you: lack of caffeine for months surely harmed the mother. This mother anyway.

I had great difficulty getting pregnant. I had great difficulty maintaining a pregnancy. During practice rounds, I had been drinking caffeinated beverages sparingly.

When I saw the beat-beat-beat of our baby's heart during an ultrasound test, I vowed not to touch a drop of caffeine until the child breathed his first breath. This was a sacrifice of immense proportion—think the Great Pyramids of sacrifice, the Sputnik moment of sacrifice, the "Tear down This Wall, Mr. Gorbachev" moment of sacrifice.

There was much suffering involved, mostly for my husband who suffered the wrath of a caffeine-deprived first-time mother. I was caffeine-deprived for months, and I was not happy about it. I'm sorry now for my husband's suffering. I am sorry I begged him to go out late at night for Wendy's Chicken Nuggets with Sweet and Sour sauce. That is just the way it was.

The cliché says, "What comes around goes around." My son will pay a price; somehow, someday, somewhere in the future he may be married to a woman who gets a little testy when deprived of caffeine. I suspect his father and I will laugh.

A Single Mother in Hard Times

Chapter 4

Myrtle Jenny Wilburn McVay had a hard life. Born on a farm in the late nineteenth century, she married William McVay, nine years her senior, when she was nineteen. Bill was a handsome man with clear blue eyes and blond curls around his full face. In January 1910, Bill, Myrtle and her mother Sarah drove to the Delphi, Indiana, courthouse for the marriage license in a horse and buggy. Family legend says that Bill sat on Myrtle's lap in the crowded buggy, and that is why her dress appeared wrinkled in their wedding picture.

Early in their marriage, the bride awoke in the middle of the night and found her groom missing. Still a teenager, she did not know what to do and ultimately went for a neighbor. Upon searching for the groom, the neighbor found him asleep in the outhouse; thus began the first of many family legends and the legacy of sleepwalking.

To this union of my paternal grandparents was born six children—four girls then two boys. Though he adored his girls, Bill wanted a boy. Before the arrival of baby number four, Bill's good friend left for World War I and told him, "Bill, by the time you get your boy, I'll be over the hills of France."

The fourth baby was a dark-haired, blue-eyed girl born in June

1918. Later that year the couple's third child, a two-year-old girl with blonde curls, died of the Spanish flu.

Bill finally got his boys in 1926 and 1930. The older boy was another blond who looked like his father. The youngest child had his dad's blue eyes and his mother's dark hair. This child, also named Bill, is my father. He was born with a clubfoot, a deformity that limited his ability to walk and run like other children. In 1930, this child was "lame," almost a death sentence for a rural boy. How could he farm?

The younger Bill needed treatment for his clubfoot. The family traveled often to Riley Children's Hospital seventy-five miles away, bouncing in a Buick on bumpy roads. Soon, the roads were improved due to President Franklin Roosevelt's infrastructure programs. The baby got better after several surgeries and leg braces, though he would always have a slight limp.

Children needing hospital services in the 1930s stayed in large wards. Parents left their child and returned when the procedures or therapies were finished. My grandparents received handwritten notes from the orthopedic surgeon who cared for my father. "Grandma Mac" (what we called her) kept these letters all her life. My aunt gave these precious scraps of crumbling paper to me. In his scribbled handwriting, the doctor updates my grandparents on "Billy's progress."

As a mother, I choke up when I read the letters, now tucked away in a scrapbook. I cannot imagine leaving my child in a hospital seventy-five miles from home for a week.

Back on the farm, the elder Bill worked hard. Neighbors said he set the sturdiest fence posts in Carroll County, some of which remain. Because of the Depression, the family lost what was forever after referred to as "the good farm in Adams Township." The elder Bill was by then ill with heart disease that would eventually kill him at age fifty-three.

The couple bought a smaller farm with a drafty old house, "no better than a corn-crib," according to my aunt. With help from her older daughters and their husbands, my grandmother made the house a home.

The elder Bill died in the drafty farmhouse when his younger children were ages four, eight, and sixteen. Dad does not remember much of his father, just a fleeting moment near his father's sickbed. Dad sat on the floor with his brother, playing with paper cowboys. He also remembers his father's casket being lowered into the ground at the Davis Cemetery. This image of two small boys watching their father's coffin slip into the earth has always haunted me.

My grandfather died of heart disease, probably the consequence of a high-fat diet. During butchering time, my grandmother cooked steaks for breakfast, lunch, and dinner. Butter, eggs, and lard were a regular part of the farm diet. Today, a doctor would put my grandfather on a statin medication and admonish him to change his diet.

Like other children who have lost a parent, my father and his siblings were cheated. Dad did not have what I had, two parents present every day, prodding, pushing, laughing, pitching endless Wiffle balls, signing report cards, or making homemade ice cream. It is easy to ask the heartbreaking question, "How would the lives of my father and his siblings been different had their father lived a normal lifespan?"

Grandma Mac promised her husband on his deathbed that she would "keep the farm for his boys." She chose a difficult path, trying to keep her promise to her dying husband. There was little money for extras during the Great Depression. When rural electrification came to Carroll County, my grandmother felt the connection fees were too high. She did not connect her farm to electricity when most of her neighbors did.

If the windmill did not turn, the boys, their teenage sister, and my grandmother pumped the well by hand. They toted water in metal buckets into the house for cooking and Saturday night baths. Without heat, they lived in a few downstairs rooms in the winter, continually feeding a wood-burning stove.

For entertainment, the family listened to a battery-powered tabletop radio. No batteries, no *Lone Ranger* or *Fibber McGee*. The two married older sisters often brought batteries and gifts for the children from nearby Logansport.

As tractors roamed surrounding farms, Belgian horses, Judy and Ginger, still pulled a plow with my uncle or father walking behind.

In 1946, the family moved "to town" and bought a white clapboard house with gingerbread carved around the front porch, a brass doorbell ringer, and a custom-made half-size bathtub. Grandma worked as a waitress when she could no longer farm.

Her children grew up and left home, as all children do. She lived in her house until 1973 when health concerns forced her into a nursing home.

My paternal grandmother was one of the toughest women I ever knew. She didn't stay in school past the fourth grade, but she was smart and knew how to take care of herself. With the help of her loving family, she figured things out. And she kept up with the world; she always had a book, magazine, or newspaper by her rocker.

She believed in God, family, cleanliness, and home-cooked food. She did not put up with any nonsense, and all of her grandchildren knew her values and strength. We also remembered the things she said, some of which referred to the old ways. *Poor people have poor ways. Let the drap fall where it may. Same old seventy-six. Cheap and worth it.*

Life never got much easier for her. She lost her darling two-year-old daughter in 1918; she would lose a beautiful curly-headed granddaughter to spinal meningitis in 1955. Misery etched lines into her face and hands long before Mother Nature did. In a photograph taken at the Camden Café in the early 1950s, she is not yet sixty years old. Years of hard, physical labor took their toll.

She was old before her time; yet I never heard her complain.

She died when I was twenty; I am so grateful I knew her, even for that short time. I am also grateful my parents didn't name me for both grandmothers—that would have made me Myrtle LeNore.

Several autumns ago, my parents and I visited the farm Dad lived on for the first sixteen years of his life. So many autumns had come and gone. What an eerie feeling to walk on this silent, sacred ground where two little boys rode Rosie, their pony, seventy-five years ago.

Nothing remained of the farmhouse and barns. My father pointed to a small ridge in the distance, landmarks visible only in his memory. On this early autumn day, the breeze blew gently through native wildflowers and weeds. This was a peaceful place, with no hints of the ghosts of the past.

Requiem and Release

Chapter 5

My mother-in-law died last Friday. We have returned from the visitation and funeral. She was ill for some time with congestive heart failure. Her death did not come as a shock and perhaps was a release, freeing her beautiful soul from a broken body.

Her newspaper obituary limited her life's work to four words, "She was a homemaker."

Those words are so inadequate to describe her full life as a caregiver. She always put others' needs before her own, fretting about her fifty-something son's Type 2 diabetes more than her own debilitating diseases.

I am married to her youngest son. I did not know her early life and middle age. With her husband, who died before I married into the family, she raised three wonderful sons.

I am also a mother; so, I understand feelings of worry. At four-thirty on the morning of his grandmother's funeral, I telephoned our son on the East Coast so he did not miss the early cab to the airport. Here I am, standing in a long line of mothers who "do" for their sons. My mother-in-law heads that endless line.

When she was younger, my mother-in-law cooked delicious meals for us. Once, while at her apartment, I eagerly ate two huge helpings of her delicious pot roast. She looked at me and said, "What? You don't like my pot roast?" like a Christian version of the proverbial Jewish mother. She wanted me to eat three servings.

⁓

Some rituals around death are comforting—others seem foreign and odd. The language we use in the Midwest is strange. "Laying a corpse" is a phrase that comes from sitting up with the dead at home. We call the pre-funeral ritual the "visitation" or "calling hours," terms that dress up and disguise the reality of death.

The rite of visitation is something I do not want for myself. I do, however, understand and respect how important it is for others.

On the day of the funeral, an elderly preacher offered the homily, eulogy, or sermon. What you call it depends on your tradition.

A friend of the family preached the funeral, and talked primarily about my husband's father—dead nearly thirty years. The preacher reminisced about traveling to the family home, and that my mother-in-law always "cooked for them and made up their beds for the night."

Feminists might take offense at this portrait. This view of my dear mother-in-law did not offend me, because I understood the context. She was a preacher's wife, always in the background providing support and strength.

I wish I had known her for more years. However, I see her feisty personality in her son and grandson. I understand the respect for family she inspired when we gather for family holidays. While she is no longer physically present, she is there in so many little things.

She did not enjoy the best sense of direction, nor do my husband or my son. About fifteen years ago when she was still driving, she made the 200-mile trip to our home. I worked at a hospital north of our home.

Mid-afternoon on the day of her expected arrival, she came into my hospital office with a stranger.

Lost in Gibson County, Mom stopped and told a stranger her daughter-in-law worked at the hospital. The stranger drove ahead of her to the hospital. Rural Gibson County has many dangerous, abandoned coal mines and stripper pits as well as its share of drug addicts. I am afraid to think of what might have happened; yet I treasured her innocence and faith in others.

After her funeral, the three sons and their wives got into the funeral home's limo and followed the hearse to the cemetery, trailed by a procession of cars with family members and friends. This was a sad and quiet drive, especially for the sons. We all stared quietly ahead until the hearse turned east instead of west. Someone said to the driver, "Does the hearse driver know where he is going?"

We went three or four miles out of the way, winding through the town where my husband attended junior high. The hearse turned back west, crossed the state highway, and arrived at the country cemetery in rural Madison County. The entire procession followed, falling in step with the confused driver.

The graveside service was brief. The family walked around to see the great-grandparents' tombstones. I chose a red rose from the blanket of flowers over the white metal casket.

Quietly, the sons and wives got in the limo for the return to the funeral home. At the end of the cemetery drive, the driver turned east this time instead of west, once again confused and going the wrong way. The white limo was too big to turn around. The driver turned back into the cemetery and made one last respectful pass. Sometimes, a wrong turn gives us pause as it did on that cold January day as we remembered our dear one.

Sweatshirt Weather

Chapter 6

Mature corn, ready for harvest, stands in neat, geometric rows in Indiana fields. The Hoosier sky has gray clouds outlined in an almost black line etched against a blue-green sky. Sometimes the clouds look surreal, as if painted with oil tempura on an elegant and forgiving canvas.

I am born again every October. The tenth month of the year is my month. Some find the season of autumn depressing, as annual vegetation withers and dies. I am just the opposite. October's sights and sounds fill my senses and soul.

In northern Indiana where I grew up, seasons are more sharply defined than in southern Indiana, which is now my home. Harvest is in full swing in October, if not finished. Beans and corn are picked; winter wheat is planted.

By mid-October, it is a little chilly for evenings on the front porch. As a child, I loved sitting between my grandparents on their front porch swing at Homeland Farm in Tunker, Indiana. Our low-tech activity was looking down the country road for headlights appearing at the ridge of the hill toward the state highway.

Nearing Halloween, we might have a fire in the home's fireplace, under the mantel of custom-made tiles that depicted family history in Washington Township. My ancestors came in 1830 from Pennsylvania to Indiana. A Hoosier cabinet, a spinning wheel, the old farm bell that now adorns my brother's yard, a plow, and an Aberdeen Angus were pictured on the blue and white tiles around the fireplace.

October was also a glorious month for outdoor activities. Occasionally, the church youth hosted a bonfire and weenie roast in a farm field, with spires of lighter fluid-induced flames lapping at the autumn sky. We seared Eckrich hot dogs and ate sticky s'mores made from Hershey bars, marshmallow, and graham crackers. The best s'mores were cold in the middle and burned on the edge.

༄

When I went to college in central Indiana, the old campus was rich with color—like a preschooler's new Crayola crayons.

My blue and white bicycle was locked to a metal rack in front of my dormitory, Hurlbut Hall, ready for use at any time. Every weekday I pedaled through the central campus to the journalism building. The east campus had few trees and many utilitarian stone and brick modern buildings.

However, the west campus was filled with trees and old stone buildings dating from the 1930s. Riding my bike on a crisp autumn day, I entered the old campus. I rode into a central green space where paths have been worn in every direction by generations of students. My bicycle tires crackled through red, maroon, and gold leaves that dropped from walnut, sycamore, maple, and oak trees. The autumn breeze gently licked my face. I never wanted the downhill trip to end.

༄

Betraying my love of Indiana in October, I moved to Florida

after college. Every October in the Sunshine State made me miss the tremendous colors of the Hoosier State. The first autumn away from Indiana my friend Doris mailed me an envelope full of dried leaves. Imagine the wonderful scent coming out of the simple manila envelope, bringing lovely, crunchy pieces of home to me. What a tremendous gift!

While still living in Florida, I came home to be married more than twenty-five Octobers ago. We married at the same 100-year-old country church I attended as a child. My parents were married in this same tiny church more than half a century ago.

We had the lovely good fortune of having a perfect Indiana October day for our wedding. In front of the church was a huge elm tree with limbs that reached prayerfully to the country sky in every direction. The mighty elm shimmered with its remaining copper and bronze leaves, that fell gently and blanketed the earth. As the old church bell tolled the call for worship, the picture-perfect day filled every sense.

❧

After my husband finished graduate school, we felt the pull of Indiana. We came back home again to a new life in southern Indiana. Because of regional cultural differences, northern Indiana and southern Indiana are almost different states. People from northern Indiana often used a pejorative to describe anything south of the old National Road as "Kentucky." I didn't know what to expect in this unknown land. That slander was simply wrong. The land and the people of southern Indiana are wonderful; it is now my home.

While I treasure the symmetry of central and northern Indiana farmland, I love the curves of southern Indiana. My favorite place in southern Indiana is around Lincoln State Park where Abraham Lincoln lived as a boy from 1816 to 1830.

A ribbon of heavily wooded highway slices through the state park and the Lincoln Boyhood Home National Monument in Spencer County. Within the park is a pine forest, which, as my father told me, is not indigenous to Indiana. Planted in the 1930s by the Civilian Conservation Corps, the trees now rise above the park and offer permanent shade.

We have stayed in the cabins many times during October, spending several days in paradise, the first time when our son was five years old. The cabins are simple, reminding me of my $100 a month apartment in graduate school.

On our visits to Lincoln State Park, we arrive with many books, board games, and food for grilling, even breakfast, outdoors. The beds are uncomfortable, the living room furniture is wooden and stiff, and the kitchen features orange plastic stack chairs. It is not the Palmer House.

Nevertheless, does the Palmer House have a huge screened-in front porch, and the combined scent of pine trees, dying cottonwood, sycamore, and maple leaves? Can you hike on a quiet October morning around a deep blue-green lake that reflects the trees and dying autumn sun?

Today is October 1st. The month lies before me, rich with unknown experiences. It is time to find my favorite sweatshirt.

Goodbye, Gum Street

Chapter 7

My friend is marrying a wonderful man. They are making his house their home, with character and elements from both families' traditions.

If family and friends designed a partner for this friend, he would be funny, creative, smart, social, caring, and romantic. He would be the man she has chosen. My good wishes for these dear ones do come with a little regret as she leaves a home she lived in for nearly two decades.

When I visited her this morning, before the moving van came, I was surprised at my own reaction of wistfulness. I have a history with this house as well.

I never had a sister, but she is my sister by choice. She is smart and tough. I really admire those two qualities. She has two real sisters and shares her real sisters with me.

We frequently disagree like real sisters, and she keeps coming back for more of my bad attitude and antagonism. That is a real sister.

Her two-story house is full of memories for me. I remember dinners with good pot roast and tiny pearl onions. Memories of kitchen table discussions about philosophy, religion, politics, social justice, food, books, and art. Memories of drinking lemonade on her spacious screened porch, memories of her annual holiday party with an eclectic, engaging group of friends.

When my son was five years old, my friend picked him up at daycare one sultry June afternoon. My husband was teaching, and I was at a conference on the far west side of our city. She frequently bailed me out. She was a single mother with two school-age children of her own, and I should have been bailing her out.

Within an hour after she picked up my son, a tornado ripped through our city. Her garage, which sheltered a new minivan, suffered the wrath of the storm when a neighbor's tree took it out. My son remembers this as a great adventure. She handled the destruction better than I would have and still managed to care for my son until we got there.

One day I popped in at Gum Street and noticed that the family's black and white cat was noticeably gaunt.

"What's wrong with the cat?" I asked. My friend and her active teenaged children had not really noticed that poor Stubby was losing weight. I did not see him every day. Poor Stubby was not much longer for the world. My question prompted a vet visit. We all still mourn for poor Stubby, but over the years the memory has become somewhat funny.

I did not go upstairs in her house for more than two years when her son's snake escaped his cage. I am not sure the reckless reptile ever surfaced—the snake, not her son. Now that son is a grown man with children of his own. His own son—my friend's first grandchild—has a pet bearded dragon. I will not be visiting them very soon.

When my friend's mother was dying of cancer, she and I sat outside and talked. Her sadness and loss were larger than the big trees that shaded her backyard. We both cried. I felt so helpless as she experienced the loss of her second parent at such a young age.

Three years ago she had a very serious surgery. She had to keep her leg elevated upon returning home, and was not yet mobile. I made her breakfast the next day. She is a great cook, and I am not. This is the high drama in this story. She survived the surgery <u>and</u> my breakfast.

A week later, one of her brothers died unexpectedly of a heart ailment. His death was one of those shockwaves that reverberate through even the most loving and stable families, which ripple outward like a stone thrown in a pond. She lost a younger brother in the 1950s and both her parents were gone by the time she was middle-aged. Her remaining siblings and their children form a tight protective cocoon around each other, even as they live all over the world. They communicate frequently with love and passion in a Google group. She is at the heart of this large, loving family.

Throughout all of her life, her home has been a warm, steady anchor for her family and friends. If she is at home, the back door is open. Sometimes, the back door was open when she was not home. Her house has always been a welcoming place, where one can bound in the door, check out the new photos on the fridge, see which nephew is in town, and pull up to the kitchen table for a cup of hot coffee.

Au revoir, Gum Street. I'll miss you.

The Rhythm of Saturday

Chapter 8

Saturday is my favorite day of the week. I love the no-hurry pace of the day. We no longer have Saturday kid-related events, and we are beyond the endless school activities and fundraisers

Today will be a spectacular day, filled with the joy of mundane chores.

My husband still sleeps peacefully beside me. This is unusual as he often gets up before I do. For some reason, the cat chose to sleep in our son's room and left us alone. Our cat Fala generally snores loudly all night at the foot of our bed and wakes us early when he is hungry. Apparently, I was also not snoring at my usual noisy level last night, as my husband enjoyed sleeping in with no cat and no snoring.

I woke up several hours after the weekday alarm normally goes off.

I make the coffee and put out juice. We read the papers and fiddle on our laptops. Off to do the Saturday errands. My husband proclaims me the "Mayor of Dorkytown" for my selection of a decades-old shirt, green pedal pushers, and Tasmanian devil high-top tennis shoes accented by pink socks. I acknowledge that the term "pedal pushers" went out with Mamie Pink and Metrocal.

The slow, meandering visit to the grocery store with no list is probably a mistake. Shopping with no list is the reason why we have fourteen bottles of Kraft Italian salad dressing.

After spending too much at the store, we come home and awaken the college boy. Rather, my husband goes downstairs to our former guest room where college boy has been sleeping this summer. My husband hears "ahhhh, glahhh, blahhhh, ohhhh." This is teenage language for "Do I really have to get up this early? It's only noon."

"It's alive!" I proclaimed as the mumbling Frankenstein boy-monster ascended the stairs at the crack of one p.m. He helps us put the groceries away, and we make sandwiches for lunch.

Now comes the best part of an easy summer Saturday: quiet reading or writing together in the living room. My husband reads *The Bridge*, a new book about President Obama, our son reads *The Seven Habits of Highly Effective People*, on his list of summer reading from his mother.

The esteemed Mayor of Dorky Town rests comfortably in her old green recliner, huddled over her laptop, savoring the laziness of this day.

Field of Dreams

Chapter 9

Spring days in the country hold much promise. Just shy of the soil surface are wildflowers, soon to be coaxed upward by a gentle April sun.

Soon the neighboring farmers will overturn the rich, brown soil and renew the cycle of planting and harvest.

On this beautiful day, I am visiting old friends. I brought a dozen long-stemmed red roses to share. I came to see Suzi—she is new here. The first roses are for her. Suzi lighted any room with her red hair and vibrant personality. I remember her on the dance floor at our wedding reception. She had such a great time, laughing and dancing.

There is Pastor! I did not know he was here; this is so unexpected and brings back many memories. Pastor married my husband and me in a nearby country church nearly three decades ago. A few minutes before the ceremony, Pastor entered the anteroom behind the altar and asked my betrothed, "Do you have a pen and paper?"

My soon-to-be husband and his groomsmen found Pastor what he needed. Pastor then quickly wrote his homily for our ceremony, scratching a few words on the paper. The ceremony came off without complications.

When my husband told me later what happened before the ceremony, I was horrified. For months, I had worked on elaborate, written plans. I had typed the entire liturgy, with songs and readings inserted, and made a program for Pastor. Printed wedding programs were unusual at that time; a church member copied the program on "church bulletin" paper. But, Pastor had lost the document I sent him. He was a kind and dear man, but a little scatterbrained. Pastor's fly-by-the-seat-of-his pants approach caused no problems, however.

Kirby and Neva are here, too. When I was a small child, they were our neighbors. We lived in a tiny prefabricated yellow house and Kirby's workshop butted up against our backyard, close enough for my brother and me to sneak through the metal gate. Kirby had a caged pet chipmunk named Chippy. Kirby often showed us projects he was working on in his workshop, and let us hold a two-by-four board while he sawed or nailed it. He built beautiful things that I'm sure still enhance homes throughout this farm community.

Sometimes he gave us goodies from his father-in-law Mr. Lee's garden.

We nicknamed Kirby's wife "Nice Neva," a name which stuck throughout the rest of her life, because she always brought us treats: a cold orange soda in a glass bottle, or homemade chocolate chip cookies.

Soon, we would hear Mother calling us, "Time for dinner." We knew not to tell her that Nice Neva had given us something to eat or that Kirby showed us how to use his tools. Then again, Mother was easily won over by large Hoosier Boy tomatoes from Mr. Lee's garden.

Kirby and Neva's friends, Bea and Phil are here. How I remember their lively conversations! There's Scotty and Doris and Kenny and Chris. The names are all familiar. Doris was my Sunday school teacher when I was six years old. She suggested the children in her class invite our neighbors; I asked Kirby and Neva who joined our church and

The Luxury of Daydreams

became active members. I was quite the zealous missionary in first grade.

The century-old brick St. John's Lutheran Church where I was baptized, confirmed, and married is just over the hill. The light blue sky outlines St. John's and a neighboring church with spires that have towered above these rural fields for more than one hundred years. Members of my family have worshipped in both sanctuaries, attended Sunday school in the church basements, and washed dishes in the parish hall kitchens.

All of these loved ones are on my mind on this quiet April morning, their places marked in gray and black marble.

If it takes a village, this was my village.

I remember their voices, their laughter, and their love when they were playing euchre or making homemade ice cream or reading the Psalms at the church. However, the voices, the laughter, the love—they are not here in this field where I leave roses of remembrance.

Only their memories exist here, memories ebbing and flowing with the seasons grounded in the rich brown earth of Whitley County. They are not here—the stones are rolled away.

After the Sabbath, at dawn on the first day of the week, Mary Magdalene and the other Mary went to look at the tomb.

There was a violent earthquake, for an angel of the Lord came down from heaven and, going to the tomb, rolled back the stone and sat on it. His appearance was like lightning, and his clothes were white as snow. The guards were so afraid of him that they shook and became like dead men.

The angel said to the women, "Do not be afraid, for I know that you are looking for Jesus, who was crucified. He is not here; he has risen, just as he said. Come and see the place where he lay. Then go quickly and tell his disciples: 'He has risen from the dead and is going ahead of you into Galilee. There you will see him.' Now I have told you."

So the women hurried away from the tomb, afraid yet filled with joy, and ran to tell his disciples. Suddenly Jesus met them. "Greetings," he said. They came to him, clasped his feet and worshipped him. Then Jesus said to them, "Do not be afraid. Go and tell my brothers to go to Galilee; there they will see me." Matthew 28: 1-10

The Pizza Boy

Chapter 10

Exhausted from a hectic workweek, we ordered pizza. Cheese with tomatoes for me, vegetarian with pineapple for my husband.

The pizza boy drove an old beat-up white station wagon. I opened the front door to meet him, and was stunned to discover it was Neil. Since his mother's funeral, I've only seen him one time.

We invited him in and I asked if I could hug him. It felt so good to wrap my arms around this young man I've known for his entire life. My husband grabbed his hand, shook it, and held onto his arm.

The boy looked good—lean and healthy—with a little peach fuzz on his face. He stood six inches taller than the last time we saw him.

Neil bounded into the kitchen and asked me if I could hug him again. I asked him about his family; beyond that there wasn't much to say.

His mother died of cancer three years ago next month. Her life and death touched everyone in our church family. She was—like many strong women leaders in a church—a thread that wove us together. When she died, the fabric of the group unraveled.

Upon her death, I promised Neil I would look out for him, and I have not.

It was an empty promise, not intended to be broken, but a vow made of fear. What could a fifty-year-old woman do for a fifteen-year-old boy who has just lost his mother?

When I see him I am happy, but seeing him makes me miss her terribly. I miss what she represented in our church life, but is now gone. I left that church for more than two years. When Neil's mother died, my son left for college, my mother was diagnosed with dementia, and I lost my corporate job, I lost my spiritual center for a while. Seeing him reminded me of that.

How selfish of me to think only about my losses when his are so great.

I cannot begin to fathom his losses. I cannot imagine what it must be like for him to touch the past. This young man misses his beautiful young mother. I look in his eyes and I see her. Now, with the angels, she is forever forty-seven—with her long, silky brown hair, lovely complexion, wicked sense of humor, and hearty laugh.

༄

Two months before her eventual death she nearly lost the battle for life. With friends and relatives praying over her at the cancer hospital in Ohio, she rallied. I was not present—I took my son and Neil to church camp.

That summer, Neil knew his mother was dying. My son knew his friend's mother was dying, and I knew my friend of many years was dying. What did we do? We did what she wanted us to do, which was to live life normally.

Over several years, we had shared rides to camp and Boy Scout events. I packed the boys' camping clothes and gear; we went to camp, just as we had done a dozen times before. North to hilly Brown

County, the camp was a cool and restful place away from hospitals and leukemia.

When Neil came home from camp and after her rally, my friend packed her medical pumps and family and made one last trek to a South Carolina beach. They took her wheelchair and everything she needed and had a family week on the beach. I have a picture of her from that trip. She is so radiant and beautiful. It is difficult to imagine that leukemia was destroying her body.

The following week she returned to the Ohio cancer hospital and soon went back on a ventilator. After a few days, she was losing the battle with cancer. The family made the difficult decision to remove her ventilator and she died thirty minutes later, surrounded by family and friends who deeply loved her.

Is it even fair for me to miss her, as someone who was on the periphery of her life? Seeing her now eighteen-year-old grown-up son made me realize that his life has been completely unfair. I take comfort—and I hope he does as well—knowing that while leukemia destroyed her body, nothing could destroy her soul.

Lessons from My Son's First Job

Chapter 11

This summer, the young man who lives in our basement three months of the year achieved a lifelong dream we have held for him. He got and kept his first cruddy minimum wage job. We could not be prouder.

Astonishingly, we his parents, have learned some important life lessons through his new worldly wisdom that I want to share:

- Work mostly stinks. Not everyone has a choice about having a cruddy minimum wage job just for the summer.
- You might have to apply at more than forty places before getting a cruddy minimum wage job and then you might have to share a car with mom or dad to get to your cruddy job.
- The car might be an eleven-year-old sedan with a scraped left front fender and faded red paint.
- People who are "lifers" in cruddy minimum wage jobs might have other issues going on in their lives, or maybe did not have opportunities you have had.
- Taxes bite the rear of even the lowest level minimum wage worker.
- The boss will not schedule around your high school friend's

wedding, a new movie that is out, a trip to visit your grandparents, or even your desire to do volunteer work for a political campaign.
- If you show up early, leave late, do what you are told, and initiate work, you might get the maximum number of hours and show up on the schedule every week.
- Chopping vegetables for eight hours in the middle of the night can be boring.
- Having your own money and paycheck is a good thing, even if you are working so much you do not have time to go to the bank.
- Young people with parents (two even) who pay for college, insurance, books, cars, and vacations might not be the norm.

We expect, to paraphrase Mark Twain, that we as parents will become even more learned over the next few years.

Mug Shots

Chapter 12

A root beer float in the summer has been a simple delight throughout my life. As a child, no Sunday afternoon outing made my family happier than a trip to the Dog N Suds root beer stand. We bought a quart-size cardboard cone or took our own glass jug in for a refill of the sweet, smooth brew.

Once at home, we made root beer floats with IGA vanilla ice cream. The secret to the best root beer float is *cold root beer*, a glass mug frosted in the freezer, and two perfectly round scoops of plain vanilla ice cream.

By the time I was in high school, the Dog N Suds franchise in my hometown had become a family-owned business called the M and R Drive-In. At age fourteen I was hired as a carhop for the lucrative sum of forty cents an hour plus tips.

Teenagers stopped for vanilla sodas and ice cream, all the while hiding contraband cigarettes and beer from parents and other watchful adult friends who might be sitting in the Chevy Impala next to them.

A young married couple cruised in one Sunday afternoon in their new '71 white Monte Carlo with a cream-colored landau top. They ordered two large root beer floats from me.

The carhop drill was easy. There were no roller-skates involved here—this was not *American Graffiti*, it was Indiana Graffiti. I wore Bermuda shorts, a T-shirt, Adidas tennis shoes, and a black apron with a silver change-maker around my waist.

The routine was: take the order on a little white pad. Shove the paper through the window to the greasy fry cook. Wait for your name to be called. Prepare the aluminum tray with condiments and napkins and balance the items for delivery to the car. Take the order to the car and clip the tray on the driver side window. Collect the money and make change from the silver changer around your waist. Easy.

While delivering the order for the two large root beer floats, I tipped the tray too far forward when attempting to hook the yellow rubber clips onto the car window. Consequently, I unceremoniously dumped both of the large mugs of root beer and ice cream directly into the driver's lap. He was not pleased with the service that day.

Some of the root beer on the tray ran down inside the interior space between the car door and the window. I cannot imagine the cleaning nightmare the couple faced when they arrived home.

Poor, poor Eddie, the young man who owned the car. I knew his name because his youngest sister was in my school class. For some unexplainable reason, I was not fired. However, I did not receive a tip from either Mr. or Mrs. Eddie.

୶

About ten years later I was with a young man (I will call him My First Boyfriend) and college friends. We were going to Burkies Drive-In, a local hangout near Ball State University where I attended college.

My First Boyfriend was a young man with whom I had an on/off courtship since I was sixteen. He was a smart person, and eventually became a high school science teacher. However, we operated on completely different intellectual levels, he was a left-brainer and I was a right-brainer. Never the twain shall meet.

He did not "get" my sense of humor. He did not "get" the collective sense of humor of my friends. He was not interested in social issues and politics, poetry and literature, or the kinds of music my friends and I liked. He thought Ferlinghetti was a race car driver and Rachmaninoff a brand of salad dressing.

In the car that day with us was my college friend (I will call him Herman) and a couple of my girlfriends. Herman often annoyed My First Boyfriend. Herman was the funniest person I had ever met and always made me and friends laugh. My First Boyfriend really did not like him and often said to me when I mentioned his name, "Why don't you just marry Herman?"

On this humid June day, Herman wanted a root beer float and ordered it from the carhop. The teenager said, "We don't have root beer floats."

What kind of ice cream place doesn't have root beer floats?

"Okay, what kind of floats do you have," Herman quizzed the naïve carhop.

The carhop looked up at the wooden menu board above our heads, reading in one long breath, "Coke, Dr. Pepper, Sprite, Orange, 7-Up, and TaB."

Not even pausing long enough to take a breath, Herman said, "I'll have a TaB float."

My First Boyfriend almost wet his pants. He just did not know people with a strange sense of humor, who could carry out a joke to its most absurd conclusion. Those who knew Herman did not react in any way, but sat stoically observing My First Boyfriend. This coolness and disdain was part of our routine. Herman would say or do something outrageous and the rest of us acted as if this were perfectly normal.

The carhop came back with the tray. Herman took his TaB float in the frosty mug off the window tray and drank it down. Without breaking a smile.

My First Boyfriend disappeared shortly after that.

I considered his suggestion and married Herman.

The Sounds of Mothering

Chapter 13

Nearly eleven o'clock on a Saturday night, my husband and I are sitting in our fat, fuzzy recliners. He is absorbed in Walker Percy's *The Moviegoer* and I am on the last chapters of a sleazy political tell-all, reviewing the final moments of the 2008 presidential campaign. I am glancing at the pages of the all-too-familiar story of Palin's gaffes and Biden's malapropisms.

I am not really paying attention.

My real focus attends to the noise outside, listening for the creak that signals the garage door ascending, followed by the sound of my son's little car chugging up the driveway into the garage.

I know he has been off work for precisely forty-nine minutes and the ride home is about thirty minutes, depending on traffic. Attention to minor sounds that signal security is what we do as mothers.

I am sure my husband is not fully engaged in 1950s New Orleans; but like many men, he is pretending not to notice that our son is late. He does not look at his watch every two minutes, or get up and nervously look out the window. But, I know my husband; he is fully aware of the hour.

How strange that I listen for these sounds of safety when my child has been away at college for two years. I have no idea what he does in his city a thousand miles away during the school year.

He is home for the summer and one of the lucky college kids to get a summer job.

∽

When we first brought our son home from the hospital twenty-plus years ago, I listened to practically every breath. I could not bear to be away from him those first precious weeks. When we put him in his crib, we listened to his steady breathing on a blue and white Fisher-Price baby monitor from fifteen feet away.

As he grew, there were other sounds to monitor. He was developmentally delayed, so he did not speak until he was four years old. I could tell by his grunts, groans, laughs, and cries the havoc he wreaked in another room—the tower of blocks that fell, the Lincoln logs rolling in every direction, the repetitive string-pulling of my prized Chatty Cathy doll that I regrettably gave him.

Poor Chatty—she lost her head twice in her lifetime. The first time her face melted into an amalgam of beige plastic in 1964 at the Indiana Dunes. I left her face up in the car's back window. My father found a Doll Hospital in Fort Wayne and she was given a new lease on life. When my son became her keeper, he enjoyed dragging her around by her curly black hair. She didn't last long under these harsh conditions.

∽

As a child with autism spectrum disorder who gained language late, our son was very aware and reacted strongly to sound. We bought aisle seats close to the stage for *Sesame Street Live*, not suspecting that the familiar "Sunny Day" theme would knock him out of his seat when blasted in an auditorium full of children. Rookie mistake.

The Luxury of Daydreams

He rode the yellow bus to special education classes until second grade, and I could hear the bus round the corner of St. Cathcrine a block away. His father or I grabbed his backpack, zipped his little corduroy red plaid-lined coat and took him outside to the bus.

When he was old enough to play outside alone, I could sort out the echo of his tricycle bell against the other outside noises. I knew if he was too far away.

After second grade, he transitioned from special education into the regular classroom.

The daily school bell ringing brought other sounds into our lives. He joined band in junior high, and we bought a baritone horn for him on the "lease to buy" plan. The terms of this are familiar to many band parents.

Pay a monthly fee for two years longer than your child will play the instrument.

Then, it will stay in a corner of your basement, as you hope some future grandchild will have the correct embouchure.

Junior high has its own special sounds with your child practicing his baritone horn for an hour a day. There's the widely attended all-school, multi-hour junior high band concert. Each year I bought a CD of the concert for $15, and they remain in the baritone case in the basement for future reference.

In junior high, our son was old enough to be outside in the pool with his best friend and neighbor. I called them Goober and Gomer. They spent countless hours in the pool playing water games like Marco Polo, and bopping each other on the head with pastel Styrofoam noodles. From inside the house, we could hear their happy laughter, and we could feel the house shake when one of the dripping, slippery boys slammed the basement door.

In high school, the sounds changed again. Frantic running up and down the basement stairs as he juggled multiple priorities. Frequent phone calls. The scraping sound the first time he tried to back the car out of the garage.

My husband is correct. I should have been standing in the driveway, providing directions. Instead, from the adjacent kitchen, I heard the retch-worthy sound of metal against the side of the garage door. Rookie mistake.

I still listen. I worry and I listen more. In six weeks, all will be quiet in this nest again, and I will conjure sounds in my head.

I'm Deaf and Dying

Chapter 14

Hope

Hope is the thing with feathers
that perches in the soul,
and sings the tune-without the words,
And never stops at all,
and sweetest in the gale is heard;
and sore must be the storm
that could abash the little bird
that kept so many warm.
I've heard it in the chillest land,
and on the strangest sea;
Yet, never, in extremity,
It asked a crumb of me.
- Emily Dickinson © 1891 public domain

Hope and encouragement are two of the most powerful words in our language. I meditate on these words, as I am aware of friends and family working through extreme difficulties.

Sometimes, all one has to hang on to is the life raft of hope. Armchair philosophers like to ponder the "why" of something happening. Numerous books cover the subject.

Before my husband and I married, his father was killed suddenly in a tragic automobile accident. We were separated by a thousand miles; I could not return to the Midwest. I wanted to send him something meaningful, so I chose the legendary book *On Death and Dying* by Elizabeth Kubler-Ross.

This book has helped many people work through life's endings, as well as come to terms with the transitions through the predictable stages of grief.

Shortly after his father's death, I spoke to my future husband on the phone to tell him I was mailing a book. He reacted oddly, and I chalked it up to the stress of the sudden death. Later I learned he thought I said, *I'm Deaf and Dying.* That particular book probably would not have been all that helpful.

Regardless, I have no answers on why bad things happen to good people. Many people believe that things happen for a reason. I once heard a rabbi pray at the Indy 500 race. After he prayed for the drivers in that race, their crew, and soldiers serving in the military, the rabbi added, "And God bless the Indiana Pacers in the NBA playoffs this week."

Does God cheer for the Pacers, the Knicks, or the Lakers, or does He give teams the ability to be excellent if players choose to use and develop these gifts?

While I have no scientific proof, I believe the little bird of hope Emily Dickinson talked about in her poem is in all of us. From hope can grow encouragement. For others who have no hope, we can give them our encouragement and hope may blossom.

Cynics may say this is bunk. Perhaps it is.

I cannot live in a world with no hope. Certain members of my family are Cubs fans, for heaven's sake. There is always hope—and next season.

I choose to live with hope and encouragement—the alternative is a void. The Psalmist addresses hope in Psalm 130, "I wait for the Lord, my soul waits, and in His words I put my hope."

Perhaps it is easy for me to have a "glass full" attitude. I have not had a life burdened with tragedy upon tragedy. Nevertheless, I know when I am troubled or burdened with life's load, I have found the encouragement of others to be like manna from heaven—when a card comes in the mail, a friend calls to say hello, or a bouquet of pink roses arrives.

Encouragement easily blooms into a bouquet of hope. I will pay it forward.

Cleaning Her House

Chapter 15

When we got the call that she was dying, we were cleaning her house. The voice on the phone said the doctors had removed the ventilator from her and that she was going to die soon. She was not yet fifty years old.

Garry's two sisters were there and inconsolable. We stood in a circle in the living room. We each mumbled a few words of prayer aloud. Everyone sobbed but me. I don't cry much.

Those of us helping clean that night were not family, but friends from church. We came to clean before Garry and his children came home from the hospital, this time without Mom.

Rhonda sunk to her knees and attacked brownish-red stains in the bathtub. Tanya vacuumed the bedrooms, in an angry motion as if cleaning the carpets could change anything. Victoria washed dishes and put them away, slamming shut the cabinet doors.

Wandering around, not sure what to do, I picked up my friend's clothing from the bedroom floor. She loved clothes. She had a huge wardrobe bought with the discount she received from the two clothing stores she managed. The year after she was diagnosed with cancer, the store closed and she lost her management job.

Her clothes lay everywhere, in boxes, over the footboard of the bed, hanging out of dresser drawers. Years of traveling to the cancer hospital a state away took a toll. Garry's boxers hung on the back of the master bathroom door.

Nobody cared about this house for a long time, and our efforts just seemed irrelevant tonight. Too little, too late.

She was my friend for eighteen years. We met as young mothers at church, and clicked with all we had in common. We wept with parental joy together as our infants were sprinkled at the gold and white baptismal font. We diapered each other's babies in the Noah's Ark-themed nursery, and we made slice and bake cookies for Vacation Bible School in the church kitchen—we taught Sunday school and took turns hosting Moms Night Out. We made seven-layer Mexican salad for potlucks and we brought our children to First Communion class. We took pictures of our kids as they grew. If someone's child had his picture in the paper for Cub Scouts, soccer, or science fair, we cut it out and put it on the church bulletin board.

It did not matter that it was not our child. We shared rides to church camp, and encouraged unhappy kids with catechism memorization in confirmation class. On Wednesday nights while the children had religious education, we sat in the narthex and argued over politics and topics of the day.

My son always wanted my friend to be the one to drive him to camp. She drove a large SUV, much more comfortable than my little sedan. While driving four kids to camp on a sultry July day, she spied a cyclist overcome with heat prostration. She stopped the large vehicle and picked him up, lifting his twelve-speed bike into the back and giving him some water. She drove him to the next town and dropped him off in a park under some shade trees. That gesture made a huge impression on my son, who talked for months about how she picked up this stranger.

The Luxury of Daydreams

My son said, "That's what Jesus would do, Mom."

Before they were married, my friend and Garry went on camping adventures in their red VW Beetle. Once, in northern Canada, they just missed hitting a roving moose. Thinking about that story, I ask myself, "Who is driving in moose country in northern Canada in a Bug?" This made me laugh, and was a remembrance of her indomitable spirit.

She was always the adventurer—with enthusiasm that sparked fires, and sometimes arguments.

We disagreed on politics. She was not shy about speaking her mind. We held our own, loudly defending our positions while waiting for our children at Wednesday night religious education classes. Our Wednesday night arguments were legendary. We disagreed about what the Founding Fathers thought about separation of church and state. We both cited chapter and verse, and in the end still disagreed, but were able to put aside our differences and remain friends.

All the young women in the church looked to her for leadership and direction, young women being a relative term meaning those with children still at home. Many of the "older women" were retired or never worked, and represented a completely different group within the church. Women on the altar care committee washed and cleaned communion ware. They made all the Christmas decorations, called Chrismons, and lovingly set out the church manger scene in the narthex each Advent.

These women usually prepared food for funeral dinners and told the "young women" what to bring. Knowing that I wasn't much of a cook, these women generally asked me to bring potato chips or paper plates.

Leukemia attacked my friend about three years ago. She did not tell anyone but family and closest friends. Word got out—she did not want it to—but private matters often don't remain private in a small community. Cancer will not stay private. It has a mind of its own.

I stacked up some books on each side of her bed. I found hangers and hung up her short, tailored jackets, a purple cape, a leather coat, a pair of red gauchos, and four or five pairs of black dress slacks. I stacked her boots in the bottom of her closet. I started a laundry basket with Garry's dirty clothes. The room looked better than when I started, but it was still a mess. Four or five large boxes off to the side were filled with random items, clothes, books, insurance papers, and an iron.

My friend Victoria needed to leave, and she was my ride. She finished a twelve-hour nursing shift in Intensive Care before coming to the house tonight and was ready for dinner. Everything we could clean was clean.

Victoria drove to a sandwich shop near my house. My cell phone rang, "She's dead," the voice said and hung up. I didn't need to tell Victoria what the caller said. She knew. We did not say anything. We ate our sandwiches and Victoria took me home.

My friend's death was not unexpected. She left Garry with two angry teenagers and a huge hole in his heart. Grief knows no bounds when children are left motherless, even at eighteen and fifteen.

For me and for the other young women of the church, the balance of power shifted upon our friend's death. One of our own had passed.

Now, we planned the funeral dinner. We made the baked beans and the German cole slaw and ordered the Gabe's Deli grilled chicken. We made the calls for the other women to bring desserts, and even found a young upstart to bring potato chips and paper plates.

On her greatest adventure yet, I figured my friend was smiling about this.

𝓑 – 𝓘 – 𝓝 – 𝓖 – Zero !!!

Chapter 16

I have math dyslexia. Numbers just do me in. When God formed the two sides of my brain, He decreed that one side be ninety-five percent poetry, words, talking, Joni Mitchell, more poetry, more words, and more talking.

The five percent of my brain representing spatial reasoning allows me to dial a telephone and add one-digit numbers. I struggle with using a calculator, and I did not fare so well in freshmen Algebra class.

Despite my lopsided hemispheres, today I called my first bingo game at a senior citizens center. This requires that I read and use numbers.

I arrived early with my prizes and already sixty people sat waiting for me. The game room temperature was a balmy 108 degrees. Most of the guests wore sweaters. This environment is incompatible with hot flashes and sweaty nervousness about reading and remembering numbers in public.

On the prize table, I put out the prizes I purchased at the neighborhood dollar store. I refer to the prizes as WPC—worthless plastic crap. These delightful parting gifts included hand lotion, sugarless candy, nail clippers, dishtowels, storage bins, a flashlight, a Groucho mask, a toothbrush, combs, a screwdriver, bunion pads, a birdfeeder, bunny ears, gum, and other eclectic WPC. This batch of prizes was of the absolute highest quality, all for less than one dollar. Imagine!

Did I mention the Groucho mask and bunny ears? My theory was these festive items might add a laugh and some fun. I was wrong.

At promptly two p.m., the facility manager was still talking with me, and the serious eyes of the players shot daggers at both of us. These folks were ready to go. B I N G O!!!!

The little white numbered balls rest in a gold apparatus, resembling a wire birdcage. The caller spins the gizmo, and six or seven white balls drop down into an open chute. The caller reads the number and fits the used ball on a huge white grid with all the numbers and letters on it. This is an easy task for those folks who are not numerically challenged.

༄

Think of it like this: some of us are good at math and science. People with those attributes are called "doctors" or "engineers." When these individuals view a group of numbers on a page, they see the theory of relativity, a chemical chain, or perhaps nuclear fission.

Others possess excellent skills in talking and writing. These individuals are called "sales reps" or "unemployed."

Those of us in the second group are fond of saying, "Which of Leonardo da Vinci's skills would you eliminate, the math/science or the arts?"

This philosophical paradox makes for an interesting and provocative cocktail party discussion, or something to ask the person ahead of you in the unemployment line.

When I see numbers on a page, I think of a Jackson Pollock painting. They look like scattered drips of paint that collectively have no meaning to me.

I blame this on President John F. Kennedy. I struggle with calling

Bingo well because of "new math." President Kennedy wanted young people to study math and science "so we can put a man on the moon by the end of this century."

That darn American "Sputnik moment" really messed me up. I started first grade with old math, and by the middle of second grade, "new math" burned past me to a galaxy, far, far away.

Forty-something years later, add to that the problem of poor vision corrected with bifocals. Did I mention my two cataract surgeries?

I spun the machine and looked through the top of my glasses to read the number.

"B, fourteen. B, fourteen."

I liked how my voice sounded through the sound system. A little like Joni Mitchell and a lot like Broderick Crawford.

Next ball.

"N, forty-one. That's N, four-one.

"N, thirty-eight. N, three-eight."

"You're saying them too fast, honey," shouted Alma from the front table. "Slow down."

I felt I was crawling along, but Alma straightened me out. I used my bifocal to read the number and switched to regular lenses to see the cutout grid for the ball. The back and forth made me nervous and somewhat dizzy. And, I have to sound out the numbers phonetically in my head. "Zero, sixty-eight."

Madeline, in the back row, quickly corrected me. "It's Ohhhh, not zero."

I felt that she wanted to add, "you ding-a-ling, what rock did you crawl out from under?"

Seven balls filled the chute. Then, I spun again. If I did not have the right touch on the wire cage, too many balls came out. I spun the cage too fast and four balls fell and bounced on the floor. I chased after them.

Everyone laughed as I bent over to pick up the rogue balls.

"I'm winning them over," I thought, assuming their laughter was friendly. They were actually laughing at the sight of my behind. Then, I said, "Sorry, folks, I have the first-time jitters."

"Move on with it," said a man in the back wearing a WWII hat.

"What branch of service were you in?" I asked. "God bless you for your service to our country."

He said, "Battle of the Bulge."

"Let's give him a hand," I asked the group to applaud this old soldier. No one applauded. The man said, "Now can you just move on?"

As the games progressed, my calling skills improved. I did not drop any more balls, but I did have trouble remembering if it was game one or game two. This is easily explained. As a post-menopausal woman, I have less estrogen in my body than the old soldier from the Battle of the Bulge. This causes inability to remember which part of the game we're in. Was it time to clear the board? Did we just clear it? Did I unplug the toaster this morning?

I made a joke out of it. "I'm having trouble remembering which game we are on. This is why no one wants me to play cards with them; I'm easily distracted."

"Cut out the jokes, and move on, girlie-girl," said the man in the WWII hat.

He was my favorite.

Each winner stepped up to the prize table after I verified the win and took a prize. The Groucho mask and the bunny ears may as well have been covered with bubonic plague germs. They did not move off the prize table.

"How about some bunny ears for the grandchildren?" I said, as two winners "bingo-ed" at the same time. Lurlene, who used a walker and sported shiny pink hair, said, "My grandchildren have their own grandchildren," and took some dental floss.

This has not been the greatest day of my life for a number of reasons. All day there's been a cold, dousing rain. I just want to finish this endless hell of a game day and go home.

Unfortunately, we've only completed four games, but it feels like I've been here since seven o'clock this morning. I know we were at game eight because I counted the prizes. I bought twenty-five. I can leave when five remain.

Wait—there is the Grand Prize, a ten-dollar card to Wally World.

Almost finished. I am spinning the birdcage apparatus and I hear Alma and her friends talking about me. They think they are whispering, but they are less than ten feet away from me and I can hear every word.

"She isn't funny. Why does she keep telling those jokes?"

I want to scream, *Ladies, I can hear every word you are saying,* but instead I say, "I, nineteen, I, nineteen."

The Third Piano

Chapter 17

It is no coincidence that my maternal grandmother's maiden name was Hoard, because I am without question my grandmother through and through. She was the family historian and I have many of her family things, going back to 1830 when her family settled in Indiana.

I ponder these family treasures and wonder which is the most precious—is it the Old Settlers Day trophy her grandfather won in 1922? Perhaps her red and blue nursing cape, white cap, diploma, and Registered Nursing pin from her 1928 Lutheran Hospital School of Nursing graduation? Or the one-piece wooden rolling pin that came with our ancestors when they arrived in a wagon behind a team of oxen? Is it the box of love letters my grandfather wrote to my grandmother during their courtship in 1930 and early 1931?

Or is it the treasures of my own life? My fifty-dollar wedding ring? The little yellow knitted hat my son wore home from the hospital that his dad and his Uncle Tony wore when they were babies? My well-worn *Favorite Poems Old and New for Children* from the Sandy Book Store in Clearwater, Florida?

All of these items are priceless to me, but one item in my home sticks out above the others, and that is my spinet piano, my third piano.

My first piano was literally a baby grand; I was a baby (age two) and it was a toy, a red wooden piano with real keys. My second piano was a loaner from my paternal grandmother, or so I thought. When I was about ten years old, my parents decided I had a promising future in music. My father, uncles, and adult male cousins loaded up the vintage upright grand piano into a truck and drove it the ninety miles from my grandmother's house to ours.

At ten years old, one doesn't fully appreciate family politics, nor does one appreciate the word "vintage." This piano was a monster, albeit a beautiful monster. A dark wood (probably cherry or mahogany) the antique piano stood about six feet high with intricate carvings on the cabinet face, and large claws on two front legs. The damper pedal required a ten-year-old to lift her right foot up a few inches, which seemed quite intimidating. The real ivory keys were wide, cream-colored, and smooth to the touch.

My paternal grandfather bought this upright grand for his three daughters (my father's three older sisters) in the twenties. Dad asked Grandma if he could borrow the piano until he could afford one for me. Dad did not consult his sisters.

I came home from school one day and the big piano was gone, and shortly after that (near Christmas) a new beautiful maple spinet piano appeared in its place in my parents' living room.

The keys were plastic, and felt completely different than pounding down the big ivories on the upright grand. I was too young to know the difference, and I loved that piano for many years. We lived in the country and there wasn't much to do, so I entertained myself with my reading, music, and writing.

I was never a skilled pianist; my joke is that I took one year of piano lessons six years in a row. But I learned enough to accompany my family for Christmas carols, and to accompany myself. Our son also took piano for several years, and gained a lifelong appreciation of music on this little spinet.

Now the spinet occupies a place of honor in our living room, next to a case of sheet music I can't quite throw away. I have an original copy of "Stardust" by Hoosier composer Hoagy Carmichael, courtesy of my maternal grandmother's hoarding. Plus I have all my own music, my much-beloved Bach prelude books and John Thompson's Piano Books.

I froze in my musical education at John Thompson's Book III—I learned the first song in the book, "Toreador Song" by Bizet and then I was done. I never mastered Chopin or Franz Liszt, just simple versions of preludes and hymns by fellow Lutheran Johannes Sebastian Bach. And I played "Love is Blue" about a hundred thousand times for it was my dad's favorite song of the time.

My piano is now a dust catcher and takes up space. I can't remember the last time my son or I played, and it is terribly out of tune. I would give it away if I knew someone could love it, but no one wants a real piano anymore. Electronic pianos are now in vogue.

When writing this essay (after prompted by my online writing group) I figured out why I kept this piano all these years, dragging it by rental truck and moving van around Indiana. These pieces of shiny finished wood and plastic and metal represent how lucky I was as a child. I had so many adults who believed in me and cared about my future.

My paternal grandmother's piano suffered a melancholy fate. To make the sisters happy, the piano went back to my grandmother's house where it only got infrequent use. When I was sixteen and my grandmother moved into a nursing home, the vintage upright was sold in an auction on a November morning and the gloomy, cold weather underscored family emotions. The piano went home in the back of a stranger's truck.

Even at only sixteen, I sensed the sadness in that loss. I don't know why no one in the family bought it. Probably it wasn't about money—it was more like the baby in the King Solomon story.

My piano gathers dust in my living room. Tomorrow I'll find the sheet music for "Love is Blue" and give it a whirl.

The Bloody Fourth of July

Chapter 18

My maternal grandmother was "a character." Grammy was always a big presence with her booming voice, striking white curly hair, and stylish clothing and jewelry. Her accessories were often purple—her signature color, long before there was such a thing as a signature color. With her gorgeous white hair, she knew to stick to jewel tones.

Her voice and panache filled any space she occupied. She thoroughly exasperated many people and charmed others. Once on a visit to Stowe, Vermont with my aunt, Grammy was mistaken for the elderly Maria von Trapp. I suspect she enjoyed the attention and did not immediately admit she was not the famed Austrian singer.

With my grandfather, Grammy wintered in Florida at Twin Lakes Trailer Lodge. Before the condominium craze, many Midwestern retirees bought trailers as second homes and enjoyed the sense of community with neighbors who shared similar backgrounds.

I was eating lunch in my high school cafeteria when a rumor spread through the group of teenagers.

"There's a crazy woman in a mink coat in the principal's office, and she has a picnic basket full of alligators," someone said.

I did not even look up from my lunch. I knew it was my grandmother. I was not expecting her at school that day; I did not even know she was returning home from Florida.

The six-inch long alligators, which survived the 1,100-mile car trip, were a gift for the science teacher. Grammy named the tiny reptiles Gus and Alice.

Every spring my grandparents loaded up their luxury-liner sized Oldsmobile 98 and drove home with the treasures and mementoes of a winter in Florida. They always brought fresh oranges, chocolate coconut patties, striped beach towels, and tchotchkes such as dolphin-shaped salt and pepper shakers for my brother and me.

Grammy's favorite stop on the way home was one of the many illegal fireworks shacks right at the Tennessee state line. She and my grandfather purchased hundreds of dollars of illegal fireworks for the annual Fourth of July celebration at their farm.

My grandparents lived at Homeland Farm, which had been in Grammy's family since the 1830s when President Martin Van Buren signed the deed. The Cape Cod-style farmhouse, built around 1916, replaced the original house after a fire. The original house burning was a terrifying memory for my grandmother and her sisters.

By the early 1960s, the "new" house had a massive front yard highlighted by a beautiful willow tree and several large pine trees. The front of the house had a screened-in front porch with a massive wooden swing at one end.

The slate gray house sat in the middle of the farmlands worked for generations by my ancestors. On an early July day the knee-high corn crop butted up to the yard. For my grandfather, its current caretaker, it was a great place to watch and inspect the crop. As the sun dipped behind the horizon, my brother, cousins, and I caught fireflies and put them in glass Jif peanut butter jars. Sometime later, perhaps a few hours, the fireflies lighted no more.

Every Fourth of July, Grammy coerced my father to set off the fireworks in front of neighbors, friends, and family. My father, who was a reasonable, sensible, law-abiding high school teacher, wanted nothing to do with the ignition and firing of the celebratory bombs over the cornfields surrounding the rural village of Tunker.

My grandfather simply hid from Grammy in plain sight, with his hands in his pockets, chattering about this year's crop and talking up a game of euchre for later with the neighbors.

The annual argument ensued over who would shoot off the rockets. For the sake of peace, my father grabbed matches and a black TV tray for use as a launching pad. He shot off a variety of colorful and illegal fireworks in the direction of the Tunker Store. He lighted each one carefully, made sure the rocket's trajectory was clear, and then quickly bolted from the homemade launch pad.

My normally reasonable, steady father screamed like a fourteen-year-old girl as he ran back from the blast site. No one was harmed. He swore he would never do it again.

Neighbors brought lawn chairs and blankets, and the brilliant showcase went off without incident for twenty minutes, rivaling the big show at the county fairgrounds.

Two scheming children decided to spice up the evening after playing with sparklers, bottle rockets, and magic black snakes on the blacktop driveway. While I will not identify names, let us just say that one of these scheming children was my cousin Mel, visiting Homeland Farm from Massachusetts with his parents and brothers.

Mel and the other child decided to melt a red candle all over Mel's hand. The dripping crimson wax dried quickly, did not burn Mel (much), and appeared as an awful flesh wound. The Unnamed Perpetrator provided the right amount of hysteria. Dragging her cousin by the arm, the child ran to their grandmother, who also happened to be a registered nurse, and experienced in the identification of burns and flesh wounds.

With the innocence of Polly Purebred alerting the Royal Canadian Mounties of terror on the railroad tracks, the Unnamed Perpetrator tried to convince Said Grandmother of Cousin Mel's serious injury.

The Nameless Child might have had a slight aptitude for overblown hysteria, which she eventually outgrew at about age forty.

Having not just "fallen off the turnip truck" as the natives say, Grammy did not fall for the melodrama. Dare I say it; she smacked Cousin Mel and the Nameless Child with a rolled-up copy of *The Saturday Evening Post*. Thus, ended the tale of the Bloody Fourth of July.

Through a Glass, Darkly

Chapter 19

Children view the world through their own lenses—colors and shapes grounded in their own reality. Like the twist of a kaleidoscope, memory changes its patterns as we age.

Our view is sometimes clear, with a rush of sounds and sights from long ago. If we are lucky, we leave the dark memories behind and savor the richness of the joyful ones.

As a person who is often introspective, my kaleidoscope of memory twists and turns at the oddest times. I confess I will sometimes drive past a familiar spot, while in my head I am somewhere else. Sometimes a song on the radio or the smell of lilac or a blaze of color will pull me back in time, distracting me from the present. I could drift to yesterday or a moment forty years ago. I choose to follow these pictures in my mind; I want to see where these memories take me.

In the summer of 1971, WLS radio Chicago blasted from every kid's AM radio in my hometown. Three Dog Night's album *Naturally*, released the year before, still received much airplay. "Joy to the World" played multiple times a day. When I hear this song today, I am drawn back to early summer afternoons, and the full promise of many lazy days until school started again.

I was thirteen and it was an afternoon in early June, a good day for ice cream with friends. I rode my bike the mile from home and found friends standing in line at Carol's Corner, which still operates today. A radio boomed the Three Dog Night classic as I propped my bike up against the yellow-painted building. My friends and I stood on the street corner, talking. The town's only stoplight hung yards away, and regulated the "lake traffic" which tripled our population in the summer.

We talked about starting high school in the fall. We would be the first freshmen in the building, one of the many new consolidated high schools in Indiana that autumn. We talked about who was invited to a popular girl's party the next Friday. One of the girls celebrated her fourteenth birthday that day. We lined up for our soft-serve ice cream and cherry sodas.

The air horn at the fire station a block away, which blew at noon every day, startled us out of a peaceful, lazy summer afternoon. Why was the fire horn going off at two-thirty in the afternoon? Soon, the flashing blue orb near the traffic signal flashed, and volunteer firefighters from all over the community raced through the intersection in their trucks. In their homes, on their farms, and at their places of work, men heard their own signals and raced to the fire station.

Within ten minutes, the town's lone red fire truck raced away from us, a group of teenagers standing with gaping mouths near the ice cream shop.

Nothing to do here but gawk at passing cars; I got on my bike and peddled the mile north to my home.

Within hours, everyone in town knew what had happened. Surrounded by dozens of other children, a fifteen-year-old boy dived into a local pond, hit his head on a rock and drowned. In the days before EMS and EMTs, the firefighters tried to resuscitate the young man for what seemed like hours. The young man did not make it.

In a small town everyone knows everyone else. The young man was the boyfriend of one of the young girls who had been standing in front of the ice cream place.

I was unable to fully comprehend this young man's death for many years. I know now what I did not know then, that life is precious and fragile and we are not immortal. I was too immature to grasp the immensity of the loss of this athletic, handsome, bright young man, gone too soon. What a devastating loss for his parents and those who loved him. What must the fourteen-year-old girl—the one who wore his school ring on a chain around her neck—have felt? What about his friends who were with him at the pond, unable to save him?

If he was alive today the young man would be in his mid-fifties. I remember reading his mother's obituary not too long ago in my hometown paper. The teenagers who stood at the corner are now mothers and grandmothers.

WLS Chicago continued to be the soundtrack of my teenage years. The boy who died did not get to play on our school's first varsity football team, go to the prom, or graduate from the new high school. Anytime I hear the familiar beginnings of the Three Dog Night song, I think of his parents and the inconceivable loss of their beautiful child.

I twist the kaleidoscope and all the patterns change again.

The Trip to Rowena

Chapter 20

Throw your dreams into space like a kite, and you do not know what it will bring back, a new life, a new friend, a new love, a new country.
Anaïs Nin

Where do dreams come from? Are they a chemical reaction in the brain? Are they divine? Are they visions, like those spoken of by Old Testament prophets?

Several dreams I've had were more like visions and less like dreams. I felt as if I was being led in a spiritual direction or hearing a message. I do not often remember my dreams clearly. Those I remember are usually vivid in all the senses. Last week I had a dream so dramatic I am still clinging to the memory, and weaving together pieces of meaning.

Weeks after my maternal grandmother, LeNore Hoard Enz, died, I had a profound dream that has stayed with me until today. My grandmother's mind left in bits and pieces. By the time I was in my thirties, she was lost in the ether of dementia.

Grammy died within hours of Richard M. Nixon, one of her Republican paramours. Having seen the movie *Defending Your Life*, I've always envisioned the two of them together on a red bus, journeying who knows where in the afterlife.

In the dream after her death in 1994, my grandmother swam with dolphins in the Gulf of Mexico off Clearwater Beach, Florida. This particular section of north Clearwater Beach was always a special place for both of us. I first visited as an infant in March 1958, and lived near there in the 1980s. She lived there during the winter from the 1950s until the mid-1980s. This area of the beach had a decades old bathhouse with wide white-washed porches all around; dive-bombing seagulls relentlessly attacked children eating popcorn. Waves rolled in to white, crystalline beaches near a long fishing pier, generally populated by locals. Tourists stayed farther south where the hotels were.

Grammy was smiling at me in the water, and wearing an old-fashioned royal blue swimsuit that I remember from her closet in Clearwater. The details of the dream are insignificant. What remains is that I awoke with a tremendous feeling of solace for her. My Christian faith offers me this blessed assurance; this dream filled me with a knowing peace, a message from a better place.

༄

Recently, I had a dream about my mother that left me with the same kind of peace. I record it now to see if it later grows in meaning. My mother has multi infarct dementia. Every day a little bit of her soul dissipates between the soft space of the before and the after.

I know the day is coming when she will not know me. When I am with my mother, we are in the moment, or the moment she thinks it is. Not long ago, I spent the entire day alone with her, and she thought it was 1942. On some unexplained astral plane, I was present with her in 1942. She talked about going out for dinner on Thanksgiving Day with her paternal grandparents. This was a story I never heard before, nor was I aware of anyone who ate in a restaurant on a holiday especially during the 1940s.

For someone who has not been around a person with dementia, this sounds so very odd. Being with and caring for a person with dementia means one must live in the moment. It is too difficult and heart-wrenching to do otherwise.

The grief over dementia happens along the way, as one walks the journey with your loved one. When my grandmother died after more than eight years of this disease, most of the grief had ebbed and her family was able to celebrate her life.

The members of my immediate family all deal differently with the decreasing mental ability of mother. My father as her 24/7 caregiver has an impossible, unending task which he undertakes with love. As she declines, he finds more creative ways to engage her. They take a class together—the women work on memory-building activities, and the men talk about caregiving challenges and offer suggestions. She enjoys painting, so Dad bought her paints.

Everyone around mother is affected, including her two grandsons. While these young men are in college, they are still wide-eyed around her and sometimes not sure what to say or do.

Dementia involves a series of tiny losses—for her and everyone close to her. These may be loss of special things she did, like writing letters or cards. My mother wrote me hundreds of letters and cards in my lifetime. Now, she can hardly write her name. In college, I was irritated that she filled my dormitory mailbox with letters, coupons, and clippings.

Last summer I dropped to my knees to see her perfect elementary teacher handwriting on the bottom of my birthday card. I am certain my father had her practice before she signed it. The gift of the card was, of course, from my loving father who knew the importance to me of birthday cards.

In my dream last week, my mother and I—at our present ages—had been told by someone unseen to walk to a town called Rowena. The only Rowena I have ever heard of was Ernest T. Bass's unseen girlfriend on *The Andy Griffith Show*. (I recently learned that Rowena was also a character in *Ivanhoe*.)

Mother and I were walking along a slowly rolling stream, about half the width of the Ohio River in a very peaceful, rural, pastoral setting. While I do not recognize this place, it reminded me of a route between Peru and Wabash on old Indiana state highway 24. When I was a child, we drove it monthly to visit my paternal grandmother in Camden or Logansport. This section of road has been closed for at least twenty-five years, replaced with a four-lane highway.

A path winds along the river's edge and wildflowers grow on the sloping bank, but not high enough to obscure a view of the river. We walk hand-in-hand, the plump, short seventy-seven-year-old and me. She walks leisurely, so I have to make myself slow down or I will jerk her along with the stride of someone six inches taller.

Mom has always moved slowly, and I have always been jerking her along.

On the day we bought my wedding dress at Fishman's Department Store in Fort Wayne, I was angry with her for taking thirty minutes to eat her lunch. My anger was stupid—and did not make her eat any faster. *Slow down, you crazy child.*

On our walk together, we are not talking, we are enjoying the view. The day is beautiful; silver, dappled clouds float through a baby blue sky. As we round a bend, we come to a small village. A small wooden sign says "Rowena." However, the town is deserted; there are no people or animals anywhere. We are not afraid. While empty, it is still beautiful, and looks like the setting for a painting.

The river is to our right, but ahead and to the left are old, empty buildings. These buildings are brick and brown terra-cotta and many have elaborate arches around long vertical windows. They are tall, about seven or eight stories, which is out of place for this small town by the river. While they appear to have a Moorish influence, I have never been to Spain, and I have never seen anything like them.

We continue our leisurely pace through this empty village, and observe four or five of the unusual buildings. Mom and I are having an enjoyable time and, as usual, she is singing under her breath.

All of my life my mother has been singing. When I was a little girl, she sang when she did her housework. I could hear her outside of our little yellow house singing *O Sole Mio* while she put her washing on the clothesline.

Today, she hums; I do not think she can remember the words, but she is always humming songs that I recognize, and many of them are familiar hymns.

After we pass through the village of Rowena, the dream winds to a close, and I never see what happens next. I am watching us walk, slowly and peacefully, as if I am out of my body, and seeing the whole thing from behind. I see a happy middle-aged woman and her elderly mother, out for a walk on a summer's day.

Built on the Rock

Chapter 21

Change frequently overwhelms me. Just when I believe I have life figured out, something shakes the kaleidoscope and the picture looks different. Every role in my life—from wife, mother, and daughter to sister, aunt, and employee—is undergoing transformation.

Considering unexpected changes reminds me of a favorite painting, *The Repentant Peter* by the artist Domenikos Theotokopoulos, better known as El Greco. A copy of this old favorite graced the living room of a dear friend, Leonila Badger, who is now gone. I often "visit" the original painting at Washington DC's Phillips Collection. The Phillips is a collection noted for hosting Renoir's *Lunch of the Boating Party*, and several famous Jacob Lawrence works.

This painting hangs alone in a corner in this urban museum. This isolation is surely by design. The painting is too dramatic to compete with other works. Look into St. Peter's eyes—you see both his faith and his doubts. Seeing this painting is an amazing experience for a Christian.

Why did El Greco portray Peter in this way? Simon Peter was an ordinary angler. Peter and his brother Andrew decided to follow Christ and become "fishers of men."

What I like so much about Peter is that he was so fully human. While the New Testament shares the story of Doubting Thomas, the trials of Peter resonate more with me. Peter often revealed personal weaknesses and needed a good "whop" on the head, just as my father would say.

Matthew 14: 22-32 has Peter walking on water beside Jesus, yet he fell in the water when his faith wavered. After feeding the five thousand, Jesus escaped to a mountainside for some rest and relaxation. The disciples were in a boat on a nearby lake. In the middle of the night, Jesus walked to them, and the disciples saw Him approaching in the moonlight.

"Lord, if it is you," Peter said, "tell me to come to you on the water."

Peter saw Jesus, jumped out of the boat, and began to walk to Him on the water. When the wind picked up Peter was afraid and started sinking. Once again, Jesus calmed the sea, and Peter again needed affirmation.

How often do I move forward on faith, only to have doubts that cause me to sink in fear?

At the Last Supper, Peter does not want Jesus to wash his feet because he does not feel worthy. Jesus does it anyway. Peter fully realizes what Jesus means and asks him to wash "not just my feet but my hands and my head as well." (John 13:9) Again, Peter—being human—feels undeserving. However, when he opens himself up to trusting Jesus, then he fully understands and welcomes the fellowship, camaraderie, and love in the form of foot washing. This is the ultimate story of servant leadership, a term that has now become a business cliché. In this sense, I know what it means. Can I live this way? I am not sure. Many cannot.

Peter denied Jesus three times on the night before Good Friday, which Jesus predicts in Matthew 26. Sure enough, Peter denies Jesus, but he also later admits three times that he loves Jesus.

Peter later sees the risen Christ in the tomb. He is also present at the Transfiguration. Christian tradition says the Emperor Nero had Peter crucified upside down, several years after the horrific Roman fire of AD 61. Peter was the first pope of the Roman Catholic Church.

Theologians argue over whether the roots of his name mean "rock" or "pebble." To me it does not matter. I find Peter's example as a human—good and bad—helpful in my personal faith walk. Peter had both the man Jesus Christ and the risen Christ in front of him, in flesh, in bone, in soul, in Spirit with a capital S, and he still had fears and doubts.

Life's changes are often like being in that boat with the disciples. Christ is out there safe on the waters and all I can feel and hear is the wind. Am I not looking for Jesus at all? Am I so distracted by other things that I fail to see Him, in the water or safe on the horizon?

Pebble or rock, Peter became a martyr for his faith. Despite his human frailties, Peter dealt with the human questions because of his personal relationship with Jesus. Built on the rock, the Church doth stand.

Working on Christmas Eve

॰ॡ॰

Chapter 22

On Christmas Eve 1983, he found himself on the night shift, mopping the sixteen surgical suites at Florida's fourth largest hospital. Outside it was a starry, beautiful, and cool evening. Large vertical strings of lights formed a Christmas tree shape that could be seen across Clearwater Bay. The palm trees swayed a little in the wind of the unusually crisp evening.

Herman didn't see any of this. He was in the hospital basement, cleaning surgery suites. Not that he so much minded; it could have been worse. He could have been cleaning the hospital laundry, a job that even in December was so steamy his gray Dickies uniform would stick to his skin. He had not been assigned to the laundry for a while, and he was grateful. The huge industrial dryers ran all night long, making the inside of the building unbearably hot and humid.

Herman was Pop's assistant. Pop was a balding Jamaican immigrant who spoke excellent English and was a long-time employee of the housekeeping staff. Pop gave the orders and taught his charges how to use the equipment. The cleaning equipment was ordinary, except for the automatic Wet Vac. Herman carried his hose on his lemon yellow mop cart. When the mop and wringer did not suck up a spill of multicolored bodily fluids, he plugged the hose into the wall and the foul puddle disappeared in a whoosh.

AIDS was a new concern in the health community. Universal precautions were not yet universal. Sometimes the housekeepers wore a rudimentary Haz-Mat suit for a particularly bloody job. Usually, the two housekeepers sported green scrub caps and shoe covers worn by all medical personnel. All housekeepers wore steel-toed shoes the color of brown mustard.

The surgical suites in the hospital basement took an entire shift to clean, from 10 p.m. until six a.m. with a dinner break at two a.m. On any random evening, several suites filled for emergencies; women needing Caesarian sections, victims of boating or car accidents, or patients requiring urgent appendectomies. Used suites needed to be cleaned and disinfected again before daylight.

Herman was low man, with less tenure than Joe or Jack from the islands, and Petar, from Croatia. Joe and Jack sometimes got angry when people did not understand their heavily accented broken English.

The supervisor always paired Herman with Pop, because they worked well together.

Petar, who had been a chess champion in Croatia, was unable to find work as a teacher when he immigrated to this country. He ended up at the hospital, and the supervisor generally had him working alone. Petar was a genius, spoke many languages, and was familiar with all the great books of the world. Herman enjoyed talking to him when their break times meshed.

In December 1982, Herman left his home in Indiana and came to Florida to be with me. He had a '73 blue Pontiac Lemans, a suitcase full of T-shirts and jeans, a pair of Adidas tennis shoes, and K-Mart wingtips he had bought for his father's funeral the month before. He had boxes of books, an Olympic electric typewriter, his Bob Seger, ABBA, and

Billy Joel albums, and a framed college degree. His possessions barely filled the Pontiac's trunk.

Morning had not come to all Americans, even as Ronald Reagan decreed it. A recession caused manufacturing plants like International Harvester to close. Loss of major manufacturing jobs rippled throughout the Midwestern economy.

Indiana newspapers took a huge hit. Herman, who had a double major in English and journalism, lost his reporter job. Three months later his father died in a car accident which left his mother severely injured.

While it was a difficult decision for him, Herman believed it was time for a new life. I had left Indiana the year before, and he wanted to be with me.

That is how he found himself in a gray janitor's uniform and mustard brown steel-toed shoes scrubbing surgery suites in the gruesome basement of this Tampa Bay area hospital on Christmas Eve. The work was physical, hot, and hard. The housekeeping staff often had to move things around. Most surgical suites have everything mobile except the lights. Carts, beds, and equipment trays were moved for cleaning.

There were three additional surgeries on Christmas Eve, so there were three more suites to clean. One was particularly bloody from an accident victim. Pop and Herman worked in tandem, and Pop whistled "God Rest Ye, Merry Gentlemen" under his breath.

At break, Herman ate his ham and cheese sandwich from his lunch box, and read a Jack London paperback he had stuffed in his rear pocket. In a sense, Herman was experiencing man versus man, and like London was on an adventure in another world.

At daylight, he walked to the gravel parking lot and drove the Pontiac home. I was visiting my family in Indiana. Herman made himself breakfast and then fell asleep for most of the day, waking once to see the end of *It's a Wonderful Life,* and wondering if he, indeed, was in Pottersville.

Shortly after this Christmas, we became engaged and were married the following October. Since 1983, we have never spent a Christmas apart.

Who was the young man struggling to make his life better? He worked on the third shift at the hospital, covered town politics at a local newspaper, and clerked at a bookstore. He learned much that year through his experiences, and he learned that there is dignity in all work.

That next year, 1984, he did not sleep much. He wanted to pay for my engagement ring, and save for graduate school. That he was willing to do all this, for himself, for me, for our future life, says something about his character.

I often think of him on that Christmas Eve nearly thirty years ago, Herman and Pop in their green caps, pushing their yellow plastic mop buckets down the tiled hallway. Herman is now a full professor at a small, private liberal arts university. That victory is much sweeter savored over the memory of toil and hard work as a third-shift janitor.

Remembering 9/11

∞

Chapter 23

I am just one person. Does anything I do make a difference in the universe?

All of my life I have repeated Luther's *Common Table Prayer* before most meals.

The night of September 11, 2001, when the world burned, my family gathered at our kitchen table for our meal. When the prayer was finished, I added, "Let There Be Peace on Earth," from an old song of the same name. We decided that night to add that phrase to our prayer until there was peace. We are still praying the prayer a decade later.

When I was a child in junior high confirmation class, we studied and memorized Luther's *Small Catechism* and talked about theology. We were not encouraged to question the faith, nor ask about other traditions. Confirmation involved the ritual of Questioning, in which the confirmands were hauled before the congregation. What felt like an inquisition of sorts took place the Sunday before the actual confirmation. I was terrified of fire and brimstone, of not saying the right thing, of not remembering the Second Article or the Seventh Commandment. My religious education was about rote memory.

As an adult, I decided things would be different with my own child. We gave him CS Lewis early. *Mere Christianity* is a wonderful accompaniment to Luther. For an even younger child, CS Lewis gave us the world of Narnia.

I am a Christian. I walk my earthly journey with Jesus Christ. This is my decision and mine alone. One cannot make a decision about a faith walk in the vacuum of a single theology. As I learned in confirmation, *this is most certainly true.*

When I became an adult, I changed "brands" of Lutheran, and found grace and peace in the accepting attitude of the Evangelical Lutheran Church of America (ELCA). Women can speak. Women can be pastors. Gay individuals participate in the family of faith. Communion is open to all. Except for the occasional "alternate tune," we sing joyful, familiar hymns.

When my son was in Lutheran confirmation ten years ago, he and his classmates visited different churches and heard speakers. The pastor of our church was open to visits and speakers for the children. Over several months, the group visited a Latter-Day Saints church and the local synagogue.

I asked an acquaintance who is president of our local Islamic Society if he could speak to the group on September 12, 2001. The talk was arranged weeks in advance. When the horrible events on September 11 unfolded, I called him and told him "he was off the hook, if he wanted."

He said, "Now it is even more important that I speak to the children."

All of the children and most of their family members attended. Word spread, and dozens of people from the community came through the open doors. I do not remember the exact words this devout Muslim said, except what opportunities in America have meant to him and his family.

What I do remember is the impact of this humble man standing in a Christian church talking about his Islamic faith. While he was talking with us, someone ran a truck into the Islamic Center in our town and set the truck on fire. These hooligans also spray-painted foul graffiti on the side of the building. This happened at the moment he was promoting healing in his own community.

I believe there are evil and despicable terrorists who want to kill Americans and who proselytize and undertake Jihad. I believe there are groups of radical Jihadists planning evil things, and willing to die to do harm to us.

I do not believe jihadists speak for two billion Muslims.

What I do know is this. Peace is the way. I saw peace and love on the face of a small man who spoke at my church on September 12, 2001.

Does anything one person does make a difference in the universe?

Letter to my Seventeen-Year-Old Self

೨

Chapter 24

My online writing group offered the following prompt: write a letter to yourself at seventeen years old from your present age.

Dear me at seventeen: "You are something, girlfriend. You are so intense about your writing and you need to lighten up. You spend too much time composing your moony, lovesick poetry about some intangible White Knight out there in the ether. Step away from that Smith-Corona typewriter you got for graduation and get out into the world. You are leaving for college in a month, and your whole life lies before you.

Have some fun. Relax. I have news for you. Your White Knight will be there. He will have the most stunning Windex-blue eyes. As *The Music Man* song says, he will like Shakespeare and Beethoven and want to sit with you in a cottage somewhere. Your cottage will be a ranch house with noisy plumbing in southern Indiana.

He is two years into your future, but you will not marry him until you are twenty-seven. That is a good thing. When you meet him, you will still be very immature. But more than three decades from now, you will still be best friends. You will still want to be together, even reading in a quiet room or just shopping at the grocery store.

He will make you crazy. He's the funniest person and will make you laugh every day. You will love him more, though sometimes you will want to smack him in the head with a cast-iron frying pan. On any given day, it could go either way. Look at it this way; he has to live with you and you are much more outlandish than he is.

Stop being so impatient. You are going to accomplish almost everything on that "life list" you made at sixteen. Today we call that a "bucket list." Guess what? You'll hear Simon & Garfunkel in concert, only people will be holding up cell phones not cigarette lighters in the arena.

You are not the smartest, the prettiest, or the leanest of the girls you grew up with. You will eventually learn that these attributes don't matter much to those who truly love you.

You will have a wonderful life and you will discover these truths on your own time, in your own way.

Be nicer to your grandparents. You will have your maternal grandmother, for whom you are named, the longest. Right now, you call her "The Dragon Lady" and argue with her on a daily basis. She is eccentric, big, loud, and has a million friends. Guess what? You are going to turn out just like her.

At her funeral in 1994, her best friend will spot you near the bier and burst into tears. You look so much like your grandmother at the same age. As you grow older, you will come to understand and appreciate her victories and losses in life.

Work on repairing your relationship with your own mother. Now you have a typical teen/parent relationship. It isn't going to get that much better until you have your own child sixteen years from now. Your mother is fragile; like her mother you are tough. Your mother has been dealing with two very strong women in you and your grandmother.

When you have your son, your mother will help you more than you can imagine. She knows a lot about babies, and you will see her in a new

The Luxury of Daydreams

light. I wish you had the maturity to do so now, because you are missing out. Later, she will get dementia, and you will have the opportunity to spend a lot of time with her that you will treasure. That will not be easy; there will be days when she is right in front of you alive, and yet you will grieve over the loss of the person she was.

༄

Okay, now I need to lighten up.

Can't you take your schoolwork more seriously? You study only those subjects in which you are interested. Your high school math grades almost kept you out of college. You will focus more on social life than academics in undergraduate school. I am appalled that you will let your roommate attend your early morning Art History lecture for you. Later in life you will seriously regret this as you find appreciation of fine paintings to be a great avocation.

When you graduate from journalism school, you will compete for newspaper jobs with all the other Watergate-era young Turks. You have two skills, talking and writing. You will need to figure out a way to make a living, make a life, with those skills the world does not value very much. Getting your master's degree is a good idea.

Take a personal computer class. What is a personal computer? Oh, I forgot. You do not have them yet. It is only 1975—Bill Gates is still tinkering with the future in his garage and hasn't even left Harvard yet.

Finally, this is the most important: find a way to go overseas. That is going to be a big unchecked item on your life list.

While you are going to have a wonderful life with real love, a child, friends, meaningful work, and a lovely home, you still haven't been to Italy. It's your own fault for not figuring out how to make it happen. This is what is known as a failure of imagination. You could have spent a semester in London for three thousand dollars. You really need to do this, girlfriend. What's wrong with you, country girl?

That's all I really have to say to you. I don't wish to be in your place because I've been there already—you have wonderful experiences ahead. Take a notebook with you everywhere. Enjoy the journey, old friend." Love, Your Much Older, Wiser Self

Pet Sounds

Chapter 25

I am a cat person. Like Lucy van Pelt in *A Charlie Brown Christmas*, I don't want Snoopy licking my face. When Snoopy smacks his doggie lips against Lucy's face, she says, "Ohhhh, dog germs." I totally get this.

My mother, however, has a different view of dogs. Mom can see a rabid, growling, sudsy-mouthed mongrel lying in garbage along the road, and will pronounce: "Now that's a good doggie."

As a child on the family farm, Mother raised and sold black cocker spaniels for college money. Her mother helped dock the puppies' tails and groom the dogs for sale. The first litter of the "Topsy" enterprise arrived the same 1941 evening my grandfather was rushed to the hospital for an emergency appendectomy. My grandmother summoned her first cousin Flossie Glassley to stay with her daughters and supervise Topsy's delivery. Eight healthy puppies arrived—my grandfather successfully lost his appendix. Cousin Flossie was rewarded by having one of the puppies named for her.

Buoyed with her lifelong love of canines, Mom decreed that my brother and I should have a dog when we moved to the country in 1966.

When we lived in town, our only pets were a pair of praying mantises in a Peter Pan peanut butter jar. Students of the praying mantis know the female eats the male after mating. Cannibalism, not long-term relationships, is the norm in the mantis world. While my science teacher father thought this was a great object lesson, it is not the same as a warm puppy or cat.

Our first dog, Mollie the Collie, died when hit by the Whitley Dairy truck shortly after she joined our family.

Something about our second dog, Frisky, made my mother's face break out and swell. In a "character building" exercise that haunts me still, we loaded up the family Biscayne station wagon and took Frisky to her new home at the Allen County Humane Society. I still choose to believe she lived a long and happy life with an allergy-free Fort Wayne family.

While my brother and I grieved Frisky's loss, my father looked for a new pet. Dad learned a local farmer had a litter of German shepherd collie-mix pups. One Sunday afternoon we drove to visit this farm and the farmer said, "I had a lot of nice dogs, but they are all spoken for except the runt."

Adorable pint-sized Lassies romped around the barnyard. The runt was about three-quarters the size of the other newly weaned pups. Something about this particular little beast didn't look quite right. He also had a distinctive gait, reminiscent of my late Uncle Chester Brown.

Who is not attracted to the obvious underdog? Despite several puppy accidents in the family Truckster on the drive home, we fell in love with this mongrel. We learned this was his way of showing excitement. For months, this runt piddled on visitor's shoes, a real Hoosier howdy to our home.

We named him the highly original name of Shep. Mom, who had a dozen nicknames for him, liked yelling, "Sheppie, Sheppie, Sheppie Doodle Doo, time for dinner." Kibble wasn't good enough for His Highness. We fed him Gainesburgers, a popular dog food of the day that probably had more "Gaines" than "burger." He loved it and would bite his fake hamburger cleanly in half and gobble the pieces that fell from each side of his mouth.

Most people can extol the virtues of a favorite childhood pet. As my mother said, "Sheppie was one good doggie."

Shep always smiled through his big, brown soulful eyes. Shep grew wiser as the years passed. He was a good friend. On my first visit home from college, I sat on our garage stoop telling him tales of my new collegiate adventures. He listened and yipped at my feet.

His wisdom wasn't the only thing that emanated from him. An outside dog, Shep smelled like a combination of wet dog, teenage boys' tennis shoes, and cigar smoke.

Shep was no saint; he made nightly rounds of the neighborhood. He was very friendly with both Hilda and Tippy, neighbors' dogs. My brother frequently interrupted their interactions with a BB gun blast. Regardless of his sometimes-unrequited love, I am certain Shep's descendants still populate my hometown.

When I was a young adult living in a nearby city, I called my parents weekly. One evening I asked, "What are you doing tonight?" My father, who always shoots straight, simply said without warning, "We are burying Shep."

I was thunderstruck by the loss of this empathetic animal, the only dog I ever really loved. After thirty years, I still derive comfort in the last verse of "If There's a Dog Heaven, Old Shep Will Be There."

Now Old Shep is gone where the good doggies go
And no more with Old Shep will I roam
But if dogs have a heaven, there's one thing I know
Old Shep has a wonderful home

Written by Red Foley and Arthur Willis © 1933

Like Birds in Flight

※

Chapter 26

*L*ike many awkward eight-year-olds, I struggled to fit in. I was not pretty—I had a Snow-White complexion and Evil-Queen-in-the-Mirror uncontrollable black hair. I could not run the fastest or keep up at our elementary school's annual Field Day. I was usually the last chosen for Red Rover because I had a foot-dragging problem and wore custom-made laced orthopedic shoes.

Nineteen sixty-five was the year I got braces on both upper and lower front teeth. My head had not grown to match my mouth, and my teeth were the size of Chiclets. The braces looked like a chain-link fence. I wore an unsightly face bow at night, a metal and wire contraption with a huge black strap that wrapped around my head. Some sadistic orthodontist who detested children with crooked front molars designed this torture device.

My mother—God bless her and all mothers—sought activities that gave me something special all my own. Mom became assistant scout leader of Brownie Troop 204 and helped me struggle through several merit badges. Not loving the outdoors, I despised day camp, nor did I enjoy cooking, sewing, riding horses, selling cookies, building fires, or learning first aid.

I enjoyed swimming and passed the basic tests—but in my bathing cap and nose plugs, I was again a social outcast at our neighborhood pool. There was that dragging right foot, which made it awkward for me to swim smoothly through the water.

My mother persevered and looked for opportunities for my physical and social improvement. When the chance arrived to earn a roller-skating badge in Scouts, Mom registered both of us for lessons at the Happy Valley Rink. Orval, the ageless manager, gave the entire troop lessons for several weeks in early 1965.

The day of my final appearance as a skater, Mom and I skated arm-in-arm with a line of Scouts and leaders. One of Orval's favorite moves was the snake-line. Skaters lined up and skated in an S formation up and down the floor to strobe lights and organ music. Popular songs of that year included "Wooly Bully" by Sam the Sham and the Pharaohs and "I Got You Babe" by Sonny and Cher. In our white, leather lace-up skates, we also danced the skater's traditional "Hokey Pokey."

Orval was the most accomplished skater, after years at Happy Valley. He loved the S formation and relished whipping us around on the smooth rink floor while "Hang on Sloopy" roared in the background. When the S line moved as one precise body, it was beauty in motion.

The skating was fast that day, my friends.

I was next to the end in the line, with Mother on the very end. Both her hands held one of mine as we sailed along. For reasons I cannot explain to this day, I decided I had enough exercise and simply let go of her hand.

Whoosh.

My petite mother slammed headfirst into the wall of the roller rink. That was the end of my figure skating career, and hers.

People with children often speak in metaphors about the bumps and bruises of parenthood. My mother literally had bumps and bruises caused by her only daughter who never skated again. I am grateful for those petite hands that always reached out for me, even when I let go.

Hester Little Adams

Chapter 27

The daily newspaper in my home county recently highlighted the final gifts of the John and Hester Little Adams Trust. A front page story explained how the Trust left millions of dollars for Whitley County and how many individuals and organizations benefitted.

What an amazing legacy this couple left!

As Paul Harvey used to say, "Now, for the rest of the story."

Long before there was an Adams Trust, there were many informal recipients of Adams' generosity. I know, because I am one of those fortunate individuals.

As a Whitley County native, I spent my early life in Cleveland and Washington townships before attending college. The uncertain economic situation in the late seventies left many young adults without summer work. I stayed at summer school and took a job as a server at a country club.

In early summer 1978, publisher Hester Adams called my parents' house after she read an article in her own newspaper, *The Post and Mail.* The article had been reprinted from the neighboring Fort Wayne *News-Sentinel,* and announced the Foellinger Foundation awards that year. I received one of the scholarships, a grant that paid tuition for my senior year in college.

My father was a high school teacher, my mother did not work outside the home, and I had a brother who would be a freshman in college during my senior year. Winning the scholarship was a huge blessing.

That award netted a second blessing. Hester asked my father if I needed a job. She told him she liked to hire college journalism students. She interviewed me over the phone and offered me a job. I quit the waitress job, moved home, and drove to my weekly night class the balance of the summer.

Looking back on this development more than thirty years later, I am astonished at how lucky I was. Getting an "internship" in the field that had a paycheck was a miracle for me.

The dusty, copy paper-filled newsroom was where Hester Little Adams reigned over her old manual typewriter in a corner. She was a petite, white-haired woman, who suffered from curvature of the spine. Though she was less than five feet tall, she had a towering and memorable personality.

Hester dressed impeccably in a tailored suit and black, square-heeled pumps. She carried a large purse, filled with clippings and paper evidence of her interests, family history, gardening, agriculture, and home economics.

Before the daily paper went to press, people wandered into the newsroom to talk with her about civic and community issues. She was a presence at many public meetings, a little giant with the power of the pen.

One of my favorite stories about Hester is that during a summer carnival, she was nearly robbed by a "carnie" on an early afternoon near the front door of the newspaper office.

She took her huge purse and whacked the perpetrator several times and then gave him a good verbal scolding. He ran off quickly.

Within minutes of my arrival on my first day, Mrs. John Quincy Adams graciously asked me to call her Hester. She sent me to the police station downtown for a story. I retrieved the information, typed my story, and placed it on the copy editor's wire spindle.

Most people admit their twenty-year-old self is vastly different from their fifty-something self. I certainly hope so. After two years of college, I was convinced I knew everything about the newspaper business, and frankly, thought I knew everything about life. Now, I am certain my knowledge base declines daily.

Soon I had my comeuppance. The copy editor was not aware of my superior knowledge of the world and found several unremarkable errors in my work.

I was horrified and ready to quit. I swallowed my pride, redid my work, and spent the next two years learning from gracious individuals who truly wanted to teach a young upstart.

Hester could charm or scare you depending on her mood. She had a propensity to raise one or both white eyebrows when animated. However, she engaged me in her interests and taught me about Indiana and county history. She assigned me stories about 100-year-old churches; so, I found myself climbing into church spires, crossing old cemeteries, and listening to wonderful, rich stories of a shared heritage.

She took personal interest in my welfare, sending me back to my little college apartment with a freezer-load of 4-H beef.

During the two summers I worked at *The Post and Mail* I covered the county fair, gathering information and snapping pictures of the winners, both people and animals.

Hester assumed I knew about animals because I came from a farm family. Visiting the barn once a year to borrow a credit card from my dad does not a farmer make. Nor had I any experience with the ancient, square, expensive German Rolleiflex cameras the newspaper used.

The smell of a 4-H Fair is distinctive—the combination of cow patties, stale popcorn, and sweaty children. From a family with a long 4-H history, I had been going to the fair my entire life but was not a fan of the livestock shows. About half of the first fair day passed before I learned that a hog only stood still long enough to photograph if he had a pan of food. The saying goes, don't rile a hog. I didn't.

That first summer, I had no idea how to get the correct exposure from the Rolleiflex. The camera bag had an ancient light meter and enclosed written instructions in Egyptian hieroglyphics. I did not do any award-winning work that summer. Hester fielded a number of complaints from parents whose blue-ribbon son's or daughter's face washed out in the photo.

By the next summer, I had experience and a photojournalism class on my résumé. I was ready to rock and roll.

In his last year of 4-H, my brother showed well at the fair. He earned the same treatment by the newspaper as any other winner. Hester again had to field complaints. This time the photos were great, but she had to defend my shooting pictures of my own brother and his winning livestock.

What I learned during my time at the newspaper about playing fair, showing mutual respect, and keeping a sense of humor at work has been important to me throughout my career. The most important lesson for me was the role of a community newspaper. This newspaper continues to advocate for its citizens and remains an important part of a growing community. While I no longer live there, those rural journalism roots are an important part of who I am.

After I finished my two summers at the paper, Hester stayed in touch with me until her death. She occasionally asked me to cover a county-related event near my college. That she took a personal interest in nurturing me as a young journalist was a gift.

Now, more than three decades later, I write a bi-weekly column for *The Post and Mail*, as well as other Indiana newspapers. *The Post and Mail* will always be my "home paper." Friends have asked me why I still write for this newspaper after not living in the county for thirty-some years. I see it as payment on a debt, a debt I can never fully repay. Thank you, Hester, on behalf of all those young adults you championed.

What Matters Most

Chapter 28

A dear friend once mailed me a holiday gift, a fragile Christmas tree bulb depicting Vincent van Gogh's *Starry Night* painting. She told me in advance she was sending a special present. Several years earlier, my friend and I had taken a Broad Ripple Art Center bus trip to see a traveling show of van Gogh works at the Art Institute of Chicago. She knew how much I love his paintings, the blasts of color, shape, and texture that rise above the canvas.

A small box appeared on my front porch. I opened it quickly, but carefully. Held in a plastic mesh frame, the bulb arrived shattered in hundreds of tiny, silver slivers. My heart fell, as I knew how carefully my friend had selected this gift, and how excited she had been to share it with me.

As strange as it may sound, this experience taught me that giving is about the person who gives, not the gift itself. When I spoke to my friend on the telephone, she was excited to hear that I received it. She had so much excitement in her voice that I could not bear to tell her the bulb was broken.

I could not shatter her excitement over choosing a meaningful gift for me. That thought is more important to me than a million silver and blue glass bulbs. It also reminds me of how much we enjoyed the art exhibit together, memories that will last a lifetime.

When we are children, we are all about the gifts. Birthday, Easter, Halloween, or Christmas, children focus on presents, size, shape, and number. Sometimes we argue with siblings or friends. We want our gift pile to be the best, the highest, and the most impressive.

As we grow older, some material items may not carry the caché they once held. Think about physical objects you treasure, perhaps gifts you have received. What matters most?

The objects that matter to me the most are those that represent important memories of special people and places. The three grandparents I knew are now gone, and I treasure items that belonged to them and were given to me as gifts.

My grandfather, Carl August Enz, was a Whitley County farmer and Fort Wayne businessman. He kept a red daily diary to manage his finances and appointments. I kept one from the year of my birth. On the day of my birth, he wrote, "Gave LeNore $500" and some random notes about their farms. He did not write, "First granddaughter born."

Five hundred dollars? That seemed like a huge amount of money in the fifties. What did my grandmother do with it?

From that same grandmother via my aunt I have stacks of letters my grandfather wrote her before their marriage. He was traveling for Prudential around the Midwest and wrote her a letter several times a week on different hotel stationery. My grandmother, a registered nurse, was providing in-home care to tuberculosis patients.

He was not a romantic writer; the letters generally tell tales of his getting his car stuck on a rutted farm lane in a remote, rural place. As I also worked in sales, I appreciate that he had the same kinds of problems in the 1920s that I did in the 2000s. The letters provide an intimate look into a developing and loving relationship that would last more than fifty years.

The Luxury of Daydreams

From my paternal grandmother I have a shadow box with the prim, white gloves that she wore to my parents' wedding in the 1950s. My aunt preserved the gloves and a beautiful blue pin in this way. How special it is to place the shadow box next to my parents' family picture from their wedding, and see my grandmother in the gloves and pin.

While each of these precious objects contains DNA of these beloved people, the memories they inspire are what make these items special. Perhaps someday I will have a granddaughter who will appreciate these things. Perhaps she will understand that her sentimental, dotty old grandmother is passing on memories. That is the real gift—both to the giver and the receiver.

Guernsey Field Day and Other Humiliations

∽

Chapter 29

*T*alking excessively is a family tradition and sport. We're all always competing to improve our scores. My father enjoys talking, and approaches speech as if he is the quarterback on an NFL talking team, calling out play after play. Usually he is able to wear down his opponents. But we all give it the old college try! Only my Uncle Woody Roller, long since seated with the Democrats in heaven, could challenge Dad on his level.

Dad likes to repeat stories. My husband, who has twenty years less experience than I do with Dad's verbal gymnastics, knows Dad's stories verbatim. Number 22 known as *American Small Towns are the Best.*

Husband leaves library book on the roof of his car. As soon as we depart parents' home for the return to our southern Indiana home, the book falls off the car and into a ditch. A Kind Person with Small Town Values chases my parents down to return the book to my husband. Thus, another happy ending in America's best small town.

Dad likes to tell stories about me, his elder child. Sometimes, I am glad he doesn't use the computer or *Willie's Blog* would be full of stories where I don't come out looking all that good. I know he means well.

Horribly embarrassing story one

Our family planned a special western vacation in summer 1968. Mom always packed our red, gold, and black metal picnic basket as we stopped for lunches along the way. The day before our departure to California on this much-anticipated trip, Mom baked a large cake with butter-cream frosting to take along.

I don't know what got into me (well, yes, I do, and it was butter-cream frosting), but I ate all the icing off the cake. Of course, I ended up in bed holding my stomach, having just thrown up, or about to throw up.

My father, the family disciplinarian, came home from his teaching job and received the news from my mother. He bellowed down the back hallway, "Who ate the frosting off this cake?"

I ignored him, rolled over, and returned to my sick stomach.

Dad came into my room, and I lied to him and said I didn't do it and fingered my little brother for this salacious crime. My ten-year-old brother weighed about sixty pounds and there wasn't a chance in the world he did it.

Dad asked my small brother, and he rightly denied the offense. Once again, my father stood in the hallway and yelled, "If someone doesn't confess, we are not going to California."

No. Not that. No Disneyland. No Pirates of the Caribbean. No Knott's Berry Farm.

I sobbed and admitted my misdemeanor. Dad hugged me and all was forgiven. However, for forty years now every family event with a cake is accompanied by the lively retelling of my hideous transgression.

Horribly embarrassing story two

We hosted a fiftieth anniversary party for my parents in 2005, a joy-filled occasion. Many hometown residents attended, as well as many of my parents' friends from throughout the state. Included in the crowd was a tiny, feeble woman in a gray 1960s era suit.

Who was she? Ah, it dawned on me. She was Mrs. Crystal Dunn, who taught at Whitko High School for years with my father. She was a mathematics teacher.

Mrs. Dunn tutored me in high school algebra. As I have indicated, math is not my thing. I came out of eighth-grade math into high school algebra and took a swan dive to the bottom of the grade book. Having a special tutor named Mrs. Dunn was appropriate, because the minute I started studying high school math, I was done.

There were so many people at this soirée that there was a receiving line. Dad saw Mrs. Dunn, jumped out of line, and brought her over to where I was talking with a group of people.

"Mrs. Dunn, do you remember my daughter? She failed high school algebra, but she has had a successful life," he said.

That is somewhat of a conversation stopper. What do you say next? *I don't leave my child out in the rain? I've given up drinking grain alcohol? For a fat girl, I don't sweat much?*

I'm thinking about carrying a copy of my graduate school transcripts around. I got a "B" in graduate level statistics, a monumental achievement for someone who can barely finger an abacus.

Amy McVay Abbott

Horribly embarrassing story three

My parents recently attended a birthday party for twin ninety-year-old retired dairy farmers. As the local high school agriculture teacher, Dad called on these farmers, taught their children, and advised them with farm records.

While I fully appreciated the beauty of rural America, I was not interested in agriculture as a career. Have you ever smelled a dairy farm? Unlike the legend, they do not "smell like money." Many childhood friends rose at four a.m., milked cows, went to school, came home and did it all over again, 365 days a year.

When I was five years old, Dad took me to Guernsey Field Day, an annual event with judging contests of dairy cows, vendor presentations, and plenty of dairy products.

One of those now ninety-year-old twins (mind you this was about 1962) sensed my unhappiness at attending this Cow Cavalcade.

All I really liked was the free ice cream. Soft serve ice cream was then a relatively new product. This was probably the first time I tasted soft serve. This Dairy King took me to the free ice cream stand several times that day.

At the twins' birthday party, Dad marched up to the one who had entertained me that day almost a half century ago and said, "Do you remember my daughter and how much ice cream she ate at Guernsey Field Day?"

The man said, "Yes, I sure do."

I am a legend, even if only in my own mind. My only recourse for this is to tell horribly embarrassing stories about my own child.

A 1967 Christmas Story

҈

Chapter 30

In the 1960s, I was an elementary school student in South Whitley, Indiana. My primary concern each December was what presents Santa Claus would bring for Christmas. From the moment the Sears Wish Book arrived, I leafed through it, highlighting the toys I wanted.

Before big box stores, our rural village had a bustling business district. Farmers came from the country to visit the Farmer's Elevator. Wives bought flour, sugar, and necessities at the G & G Market. Many people gardened and canned, so few bought vegetables or fruit, except in December when the high school's Sunshine Society sold Florida oranges to benefit Riley Children's Hospital in Indianapolis.

Citizens visited the brick post office to see Postmaster Clarence Pook, pick up mail, and catch up on local news. Across the street, a comfortable white house served as the town's busy library with a real-life Marian the Librarian, and a Story Lady, who donned a bonnet and old-fashioned long dress to host weekly Story Hours for children.

The day after Thanksgiving, the volunteer firefighters hung giant red and white plastic candy canes from the lamps on State Street and displayed a life-size manger scene near the three-way stop on the south end of town. Snow came early and blanketed the ground until after the IHSAA boys' basketball tournament in early spring.

My father bought our real Christmas tree every year from a local tree farm. Our ranch-style home lacked a fireplace, so my brother and I hung our red and white flannel stockings on the windowsills. Mom used Elmer's glue and green glitter to paint our first names on the white furry part of the red flannel Christmas stockings.

My father taught high school science and agriculture and advised the Future Farmers of America chapter. Each year the FFA chapter raised money, bought the high school a real Christmas tree, and decorated it with blue, green, and red bulbs and fragile, sparkling glass ornaments. The school community enjoyed the tree until the semester ended.

Tradition dictated that the FFA boys and my father take the tree, decorations and all, to a needy family chosen by the other teachers. Our 1965 Chevy Biscayne station wagon was inadequate to cart the nearly nine-foot tree to this family. Dad borrowed the school's World War II-era Army truck from Willie Sims, the maintenance man.

School was out for the semester just a few days before Christmas. Dad let the chosen family know they would be receiving a large, fully decorated Christmas tree. Dad and several of the FFA boys would bring the tree to their home.

The family members ranged in age from an infant to an eighteen-year-old, with ten other children in between. The father was out of work, a rarity in Middle America then, when good manufacturing and farming jobs were readily available. There were no subsidized school lunches, free books, or heating assistance.

Dad had his students put the decorated tree in the back of the old truck. The three of them—the thirty-something schoolteacher and the two teenage boys in blue corduroy Future Farmer jackets—were in a

The Luxury of Daydreams

festive mood, congratulating themselves on the good deed they were about to do.

They traveled east on the state highway past the well-manicured farms, bright, freshly painted red barns and white fences. As the old truck turned onto a county road, pieces of packed ice and gravel spit up from the truck's worn tires.

Nearing the family's home, Dad turned around and looked in the truck bed to check on the gift.

No tree.

No lights.

No decorations.

No green and red metal tree stand.

Nothing but an empty and scratched truck bed.

Dad turned the truck around. Dad and the students retraced their steps to town where the shops were closing for the night. The twinkle of holiday bulbs and the lights from the Evangelical United Brethren Church signaled evening.

Nothing could be found. Now past five o'clock, stores were already closing, if not already closed, on State Street. It was two days before Christmas.

Dad thought about it. "What should I do? Should I go home and get our tree?"

He did not believe that was a good choice, with his two small children enjoying the tree, but he steeled himself for that option. If need be, he thought, his children could learn about sharing.

Darkness coming, the gray truck and three not-so-wise men arrived in town. A tree lot at the used car place was closing for the night. Dad reached in his wallet and bought the nicest tree that remained on the lot. Then, off to Huffman and Deaton's Hardware for lights and ornaments and a new metal tree stand. Joe Huffman was closing his register for the day but recognized my father and let him in.

With a new tree in the bed of the beat-up gray truck, the group headed east again. As they tentatively approached the family's large farmhouse, they could spy children watching them from each window. The family's older children greeted the group, and set up the tree in their living room. Dad noticed a stack of presents and bags of candy and fruit donated by the Lions Club and other community groups.

The scent of anticipation and cinnamon apples hung in the air. The teacher and the teenagers left the family in happiness and wonder.

Our family had our usual Christmas celebration. I am certain we went to our German Lutheran church on Christmas Eve, and my brother and I sang in the children's program.

I am certain nervous children in Sears' plaid robes re-created the manger scene.

I am certain we sang carols about a needy couple two thousand years ago who had their child in poor surroundings.

I am certain my brother and I ran from our bedrooms early the next morning to see what treasures lay wrapped and waiting under our tree.

I am certain my brother and I balked when our mother made us eat breakfast before unwrapping our numerous gifts and toys.

I am certain Christmas was delightful, though I cannot remember one specific gift I received or what we ate at our holiday meal.

I don't know what happened to the large family. I haven't lived in my hometown for more than thirty years.

What I do know is this: my father spent much more on the family's tree and decorations than he did on ours. Dad and those long-forgotten high school students received a huge blessing when they saw the lights in the eyes of those children.

My family receives a blessing in the annual retelling of this tale, with its message of the power in giving.

Several weeks later, Dad went into the brick post office to pick up the mail and chat with Clarence the postmaster. A man Dad did not know came in and began talking to Clarence in a loud voice.

"Clarence," the stranger said. "It's the oddest thing. You know, I was driving out east of town a few nights before Christmas, and you would not believe it, I found a completely decorated, beautiful nine-foot Christmas tree that someone had thrown in a ditch!"

On Our Way Rejoicing

Afterword

While it is a cliché, my reasons for writing have always been simple. I love words. With words, I can paint. With words, I can sing. With words, I can dance.

Like the awkward, freckled girl in the Rachel Field poem *My Inside-Self*, I have an inside self and an outside self. I was a clumsy, plain child with wild hair only tamed by a pixie cut. I had braces on my teeth and constantly fell over my own feet.

As we age, we rejoice as the two selves merge—the inside and the outside. As I grew, I learned from my parents and other significant adults that real beauty is not always visible. I did not know as a child that beauty also lives inside. We all appreciate outward beauty; yet, much real beauty is hidden. Aging allows us fuller appreciation of all that is around and within us. Grace and love gifted by others open our eyes to real beauty, whether or not it is visible. Inevitable losses chisel grace into our souls and etch wisdom on our faces as if carved from a celestial block of marble.

The quest for real beauty is an eternal one, born in real life and fairy tales. I have learned to look beyond the obvious—to see, hear, smell, touch, and taste all the richness in life.

In my daydreams, I feel the angels on my shoulder, the counsel of those loved ones who came before me, and the courageous legacy of the family farm ethic.

In the preparation of *The Luxury of Daydreams*, these precious gems of memory rolled out before me like diamonds shaken from a jeweler's black velvet bag.

Thank you for sharing my memories and my inside self.

Amy McVay Abbott

About the Author

Amy McVay Abbott is a native of Whitley County, Indiana, and currently lives in Warrick County, Indiana. She and her husband, Randy, have one son, Alexander. Amy has a bachelor of science and a master of arts in journalism from Ball State University in Muncie, Indiana. She is a Christian, a lifelong Lutheran, and a follower of the Prince of Peace. Amy likes to hear from readers at amymcvayabbott@gmail.com.

Visit the West Bow Press web site to purchase additional copies at www.westbowpress.com/Bookstore/BookstoreHome.aspx.